BITCOIN IS BETTER

BITCOIN IS BETTER

Natural Money that Works for the Working Class

DANIEL HERSHBERGER

ISBN 9798218268602 (hardcover)
ISBN 9798218268640 (paperback)
ISBN 9798218268619 (ebook)

Cover design by: Daniel Hershberger
Printed in the United States of America

Contents

Acknowledgements

To my **resilient wife**, your ability to find profound beauty in life's simplest moments reminded me that love is the most valuable currency. To my **tinkering son**, your innocent perspective — that "you can't copy and paste bitcoin" — embodied its simplicity. To my **joyful son**, your timely bitcoin drawing that you slid under my office door was a ray of inspiration. To my **wild-at-heart son**, your fearless nature encouraged me to champion the cause of honest money.

To **Satoshi Nakamoto**, your discovery of natural money and decision to recede into the background forever shaped the future of work. **Hal Finney**, your pioneering spirit remains an emblem of hope for the many you left behind. **Adam Back,** your work with Hashcash laid the stones upon which natural money was constructed. **Andreas Antonopolis**, your memorable phrase "not your keys, not your coins," protected many from losing bitcoin. **Michael Saylor**, your fearless leadership in business blazed a trail for countless others. **Saifedean Ammous**, you helped millions navigate the stormy seas of money and economics. **Jeff Booth**, you unveiled a world where technology and finance dance together in harmony. **Natalie Brunell**, your voice bridged the chasm between bitcoin and the working class. **Greg Foss**, your mathematical insights have instilled confidence in a better future for our kids. **President Nayib Bukele,** your leadership placed El Salvador at the frontlines of the bitcoin revolution. **Jack Mallers** and **Max Keiser,** your vibrant personalities colored the tapestry of bitcoin's global adoption. **Alex Gladstein,** your relentless pursuit of human rights gave bitcoin a higher purpose. **BTC Sessions,** your video tutorials unlocked bitcoin self-custody for the masses. And to the authors of **Thank God for Bitcoin,** your book enriched my spiritual understanding of money.

In gratitude, I lay down these words in hope that they benefit my loved ones and illuminate the path to natural money for others as each of you have done for me.

The Author

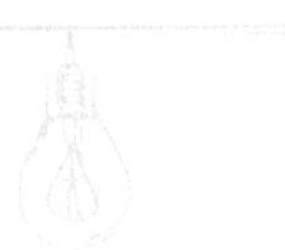

Engineer and entrepreneur Daniel Hershberger was puzzled during the COVID-19 pandemic: Why did real estate and stock prices climb while the world was locked down? He found the answer by learning to ask better questions. For Daniel, bitcoin is more than currency—it's a tool that empowers a better way of life. His nonprofit champions this, introducing the working class to bitcoin as a better savings account. His debut book offers a  fresh take on the practical reasons why bitcoin makes money, economics, politics, property, and health better for the working class. Outside of his work at www.bitcoinisbetter.org, he's a devoted Christian, husband, and father, savoring moments of golf, foosball, and bass fishing with his loved ones.

INTRODUCTION
THE LIGHT OF TRUTH

We use money every day, but what is it? Imagine I grow oranges and you build houses. Without money, how do we trade with each other? Unless you are willing to accept ten truckloads of my oranges, I cannot buy one of your houses.

Today, one of the biggest problems is how complicated money has become. How many US dollars will there be today, tomorrow, and ten years from now? The unpredictable nature of the world's money supply has made money a complicated business. The unpredictable money supply has forced the working class to hire armies of financial advisors and legions of lenders whose sole job is to help people beat inflation.

The big idea of Bitcoin is that money should be as simple as possible to understand. Money should be a transparent book of transaction records that requires the least amount of trust between two people who want to trade — nothing more and nothing less.

Money should not steal from you; if money is designed to steal from you, then you need to use better money.

Stealing may sound a bit harsh, but I can't think of a better word to describe what you are about to learn. Money supply manipulation is a silent crime, and most people are unaware that the fruits of their labor are being stolen by a politically connected group of money manipulators.

As a holder of government money, when more new money is created, the purchasing power of your old money falls. This is how money is manipulated in order to steal from you.

If you live in America, then your theft is more subtle than in other places in the world. The US dollar has only lost 96% of its purchasing power over the last 100 years. If you were born in a country other than America, you are likely to, at some point in your life, experience a 96% currency devaluation in months instead of centuries. Other countries can't pay back debts with freshly printed dollars and therein lies the ethical case for a neutral global reserve currency. In this book, I explore the tradeoffs for and against America holding on to its global reserve currency status.

My name is Daniel Hershberger. I am a family man who enjoys nothing more than spending time with my wife and children. I have been a full-time entrepreneur since 2018. Early in my career as an engineer, I led projects and built databases for large corporations, including banks. Money is a database, but it wasn't until I was locked down during the COVID-19 pandemic that I began to ask questions about how it worked.

- Why is the CPI inflation rate higher than the rate of my bank savings account?
- Why is the stock market going up during the COVID-19 lockdowns?
- If new technology reduces labor costs, then why is the cost of living getting higher?

I learned bad money was really good at keeping me too busy to ask questions about it. The silver lining of the pandemic was that lockdowns forced me to slow down and ask better questions. For you to get the most out of this book, you also need to slow down and ask better questions. It takes humility to ask honest questions about a system you have worked for your entire life.

Why does Bitcoin matter? Bitcoin is the future of money. It is a public software that is open to everyone yet controlled by no one. It has the potential to be as transformational to humanity as the discovery of fire, the wheel, electricity, and the internet. But not everyone is ready for it.

On October 5, 2009, New Liberty Standard posted the first bitcoin for sale — $1 for 1,309.03 bitcoin. Twelve years later, that same $1 exchanged for bitcoin grew to be worth over $72 million dollars. No human has ever witnessed anything like bitcoin's growth in purchasing power.

This level of rapid growth leads everyone to ask the same obvious question. Are Bitcoin's best days behind it?

No one likes feeling late to the party. For years, the pain of missing out on life-changing wealth in the past prevented me from taking an honest look at bitcoin as better money. It was more comfortable for me to dismiss Bitcoin than to ask questions about it. The truth is that no matter when you pick up this book, you are not too late to start benefiting from Bitcoin.

Bitcoin is better technology for money today. No one was ever too late to adopt fire, wheels, electricity, or the internet. All new users of those technologies benefited the moment they chose to adopt the better technology. The benefits of Bitcoin are no different.

- Bitcoin is unprintable. There will never be more than 21 million bitcoin.
- Bitcoin is divisible. One bitcoin is divisible into 100 million satoshis.
- Bitcoin is a brain wallet. Anyone can memorize 12 words and cross a border with their wealth intact.
- Bitcoin is decentralized. Anyone can run Bitcoin software on a cheap computer to verify that the rules are being followed.
- Bitcoin is digital energy. It is equally hard for anyone to create new bitcoin.

I hope this book helps you ask better questions, so you can make an educated decision on whether Bitcoin is better for you. To begin our journey together, we are going to detangle the web of our most complex topic — money. Only after you see bad money can you understand bitcoin as better money. The first step to freedom is knowing you are trapped; prey cannot escape from a trap it doesn't know it is in. To cleverly plot your escape from the world of economic spiders, you must shine the light of truth on their web. This web is called fiat money.

In this book, we explore a wide array of problems in society and imagine how Bitcoin can make the problems we face better. I am not an academic, so I am not writing this book to replace the plethora of textbooks on monetary history. Instead, I want to take you on the same common-sense, working-class journey I took in discovering the reasons why bitcoin is better money for a better world. Let's begin.

1
MONEY

"The people must be helped to think naturally about money. They must be told what it is, and what makes it money, and what are the possible tricks of the present system which put nations and peoples under control of the few." —Henry Ford, *My Life and Work.*[1]

Bitcoin is money in its most natural form: energy. This clever currency is mined by energy to outsmart the tricks of the present system and safeguard every worker's wage from theft.

A word of warning, what you are about to read may upset you. Your wages are being stolen. Resist the urge to get angry. My advice is to know your enemies, love your enemies, and get bitcoin. Who is your enemy? In this book, I define your enemy as people who want to control you.

Negative propaganda has poisoned your mind for years. You are conditioned to constantly complain instead of asking questions about what is really going on. It is time to follow the money. The money manipulators are incentivized to indoctrinate you, not educate you. It is easier to control an uneducated, unhealthy, and angry population than an educated, healthy, and optimistic people. For you, that control ends now.

When the money is broken, division strategies make perfect financial sense. Unsolved problems are more profitable for those in power.

In our short time together, I ask you to drop your political red or blue glasses and pick up a new set of orange ones. Everything is going to look different when you follow the money. The truth will set you free, but it will tick you off first. I am sorry, I don't make the rules.

Here are the important questions to ask yourself in this chapter:

- Who makes my money?
- What are the costs for making my money?
- What do I do if bitcoin is better money?

When you work to earn a type of money, you agree to the rules of that money. Bitcoin software is public code; anyone can look at the rules of Bitcoin and decide if they want to use it as money. For this reason, I like to call bitcoin freedom money. You get to choose bitcoin as better money. Unlike government money, you get to see the rules and decide if bitcoin is better money before you work for it.

The rules of government money are unknown:

- How many dollars will there be in the future?
- Who will be allowed to use those dollars?
- How many dollars do I need to afford retirement?

Without transparent rules and voluntary adoption, government money can only be enforced through the threat of violence.

Think about it. If the Chinese Communist Party passed a global legal tender law that forced you to work for their endlessly printable currency, would you use it? Not voluntarily. In fact, you would probably go to war to keep your labor from paying for another country's reckless political spending. Americans account for about 4% of the global population and yet 50% of global trade is invoiced in US dollars.[2] We explore the intertwined topic of money manipulation, war, and politics in Chapter 3.

My point is this: Everyone needs a monetary unit where the total supply cannot be manipulated for political reasons. Most people are simply too angry or too busy to realize the root of their financial problems. This is normal with new technology. When Henry Ford showed up, most people allegedly just wanted faster horses. And today, most people just want louder politicians. It took 42 years after Ford's assembly line for most American households to own an automobile.[3] The lesson here is that peaceful technological adoption takes time.

The voluntary nature of bitcoin adoption makes it slower and more volatile than a government decree, but also much more peaceful.

Instead of the winners of war imposing their manipulated money on defeated opponents, with bitcoin individuals get to peacefully choose to use it as better money. This is what Henry Ford hoped for, according to a 1921 *New-York Tribune* article titled "Ford Would Replace Gold with Energy Currency and Stop Wars."[4]

How does backing money with energy promote peace? The oldest problem with money is flawed human nature: The temptation to make money without work has been too much for any mortal man to resist. If a man can manufacture money without expending energy, then he can steal energy from every worker who lacks his privilege to manufacture money. Money without energy is a clever way for the rich and powerful to steal labor from the poor and weak. The working poor are forced to trade their limited time for an unlimited supply of money.

What awaits a civilization at the end of this wealth redistribution game? It is simple. As the value of money melts with manipulation, history says hyperinflation; prices rise and civilizations fall. From Ancient Rome to the United States of America, governments that appoint powerful people to positions where they can counterfeit money collapse their civilizations.

Politicians cannot outwit the laws of mathematics. Let's look at the example of Ancient Rome. Over a period of 300 years, Roman authorities diluted government coins from 95% silver down to 5% silver.[5] Roman politicians sucked the economic energy right out of their money. Authorities spent the newly counterfeited money on extravagance and war before working people noticed higher prices for goods and services.

Over time, Roman coins became worth much less work than their face value suggested. The flow of fake money financed government spending beyond tax revenues. Only when workers in the real economy woke up and demanded better money for their labor did things change for the better.

Inflation and the Fall of the Roman Empire

Visual 3: Debasement of Roman Currency

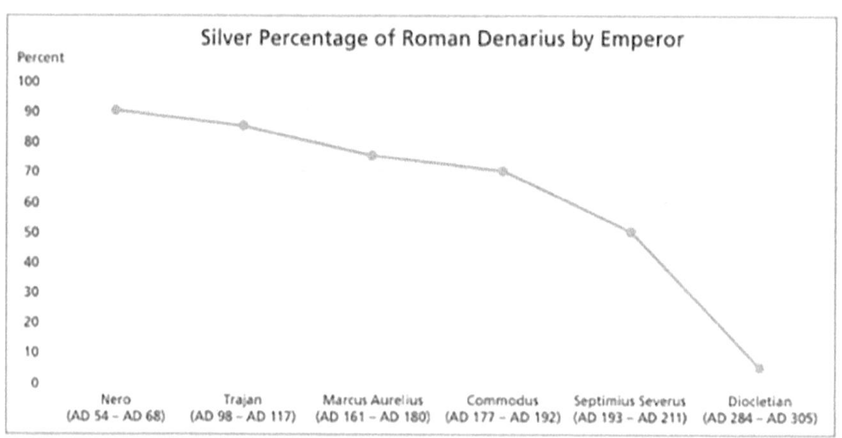

Source: Mary Boatwright, Daniel Gargola, and Richard Talbert, *A Brief History of the Romans.*[6]

The Roman political class amassed a counterfeited amount of power which was divorced from economic reality. This power imbalance fueled political corruption. The result was economic instability and dictatorship — and then hyperinflation hit Rome. The government could no longer pay its soldiers in a currency that bought a reasonable amount of goods and services. Prices rose and the Roman Empire collapsed.[7]

Critics of Bitcoin claim that a growing supply of money is necessary to fuel a growing economy. This argument is rooted in the idea that saving money is bad and spending money is good. However, history tells a different story. I have one simple question for these critics: Can you name one civilization in history that collapsed because of citizens saving too much money?

Here is the lesson from economic history. Irresponsible spending leads to irresponsible debt, and irresponsible debt destroys your nation. When we are allowed to save money, we think more about the long-term consequences of our choices. When people are forced to quickly spend money whose value is melting away, we think more about short-term gratification, which leads to consumerism.

This book will show you a better, more peaceful solution to making new units of money. The danger of debt spirals is that they happen suddenly, and power-hungry politicians never let a good crisis go to waste. The money manipulators who broke the system will blame Bitcoin.

To prevent another crisis, the money manipulators will demand more control over your money. You can expect these monetary rulers to promote cash expiration dates, chip implants, and programmable digital currencies that are fully controlled by the State. "Sorry citizens. Your paper cash is no longer legal tender. Now it is worthless paper. Thank you for your cooperation."

Who are the money manipulators? They are a closed network of political insiders who print debt to create new units of money without adding any economic value to society. CBDCs (central bank digital currencies), UBI (universal basic income), stakeholder capitalism, energy conservation, and fear propaganda are their strategies to propagate tools of control onto the working class.

Bitcoin is the peaceful protest against their dystopian idea of wealth without work. You were not born to wear central bank digital chains or beg for universal basic imprisonment. If you desire liberty, you must know the enemy of your liberty. It is time to meet the Keynesian Kings.

WHO MAKES MY MONEY?

The Keynesian Kings are guarded by motes of manufactured money.

We are witnessing the oldest of problems play out once again: A group of mortal men want to manufacture money without work. They hide behind corporate slogans of social justice, equality, and environmentalism. These kings are praised by academia and politicians as the brightest minds, yet greed is their vice. It is impossible to judge the intentions of men, but it is irresponsible to not judge the fruits of their actions.

Behind skyscraper windows, these kings run a money printer in plain sight. This money printer funds the church of government, and the church of government protects the Keynesian Kings' extravagant lifestyles. A profession that enables politicians to bypass taxation and spend beyond tax revenue is a lucrative business. Look up in every major US city, and you'll notice most skyscrapers are owned by one sector: banks.

Banks enjoy the privilege of helping politicians and corporations print their way out of the real work it takes to solve real problems. These Keynesian Kings follow the teachings of "aggregate demand" introduced by John Maynard Keynes (1883-1946). Lord Keynes suggested that during recessions, governments should increase spending and lower taxes to boost aggregate demand and thus stimulate the economy.

Keynes flipped government overspending from a social harm to a social good. His unnatural idea of debt-fueled economic growth gave rise to the need for unnatural debt-fueled money creation. Who was this father of debt-fueled economics? Keynes was a devout atheist, pedophile, and Fabian socialist who wanted to seduce the minds of young people for cultural deviation.

In 2008, *The Atlantic* reported:

Keynes obsessively counted and tabulated almost everything; it was a life-long habit. As a child, he counted the number of front steps of every house on his street. Later he kept a running record (not surprisingly) of his expenses and his golf scores. He also counted and tabulated his sex life. The first diary is easy: Keynes lists his sexual partners, either by their initials (GLS for Lytton Strachey, DG for Duncan Grant) or their nicknames ("Tressider," for J. T. Sheppard, the King's College Provost). When he apparently had a quick, anonymous hook-up, he listed that sex partner generically: "16-year-old under Etna" and "Lift boy of Vauxhall" in 1911, for instance, and "Jew boy," in 1912.[8]

My point is this: Honest money is disliked by dishonest men. Despite being married for 21 years to famed Russian ballerina Lydia Lopokova, Keynes kept records of seducing men and even children. Instead of disqualifying him from public service, Keynes was selected to lead the British government at the 1944 United Nations Monetary and Financial Conference in Bretton Woods, New Hampshire.[9]

At this historic conference, 44 Allied nations gathered to decide the post-World War II future of the global financial system. Bretton Woods established the International Monetary Fund (IMF), World Bank, and the gold-backed dollar as the world's reserve currency. The IMF credits Lord Keynes for helping to usher in the post-World War II economic order at the conference.[10] Keynes proposed all currencies should be pegged to a global currency, called the bancor. His proposal for a bancor system did not prevail at Bretton Woods, but when the gold-backed dollar system failed in 1971, Keynes' ideas were reborn in the form of unbacked and freely floating fiat money which rewards spenders and punishes savers.

When grappling on the battlefield of ideas, character assassination is one of the weakest weapons. I bring light to Keynes' moral failings and involvement in the Fabian Socialist Society to discourage blind faith in his widely accepted theory of a debt-fueled monetary system.

What is a Fabian Socialist? In 1910, Fabian Society leader George Bernard Shaw designed a stained-glass window to artistically articulate the mission of the Fabian socialists. The artwork is displayed at the London School of Economics, an elite university which was founded by Shaw and the Fabian Society in 1895.[11] The imagery Shaw chose for this stained-glass window was of himself and Sydney Webb heating up the world and re-shaping it with hammers. Above Shaw and Webb hangs a banner that reads "REMOULD IT NEARER TO THE HEART'S DESIRE."

"The Fabian Window in the Shaw Library, Old Building, LSE."
Picture by LSE/Nigel Stead.

Displayed at the London School of Economics; **George Bernard Shaw designed the Fabian-Stained Glass Window in 1910 as a commemoration of the Fabian Society.** The window shows fellow Society members H.G. Wells, Sidney Webb, and ER Pease helping to build "the new world" by founding the London School of Economics with money left to them by Henry Hutchinson, as well as other well-recognized members such as Graham Wallas and playwright George Bernhard Shaw who desired to see the world governed by a socialist dictatorship.

In this artwork, the hammering of Shaw and Webb is overseen by their coat of arms, a wolf disguised in sheep's clothing. According to author John Perdue, this wolf represents the Fabian Society's preferred approach for achieving a slow, imperceptible transition to global socialism. In this chapter I encourage you to heed the words of Jesus, "Beware of false prophets. They come to you in sheep's clothing, but inwardly they are ravenous wolves."[12] A wolf in sheep's clothing is more dangerous than a fox in a henhouse; beware of the Fabian Socialists.

To fully undress this socialist wolf in sheep's clothing, we must consider the impact of Bretton Woods on our modern world. We must dive a bit deeper to consider how this agreement enabled debt-fueled global state socialism to spread across the globe. For now, let's master the basics of money, so you can worry less about money. Thomas Edison wrote, "As a cure for worrying, work is better than whisky. Much better."[13] Like whiskey, bad money has numbed America for a night. Good money will sober up America to the truth that there is no substitute for hard work.

Money without work is worthless. To trade a worthless thing requires trickery. If truth unites us, then trickery divides us. Therein lies the root cause of money problems that plague society. The trickery of boom-bust-bailout cycles are more profitable for the people who print our money.

How does this trickery work in action? The central bank manipulates interest rates which sparks boom-and-bust economic cycles. Instead of borrowers and lenders determining interest rates on a free market, the central bank artificially sets the price of borrowing by creating new money. By controlling the price of money, it allows the Keynesian Kings to time markets using new money to buy assets low and sell assets high.

The profit incentives from an unstable money supply bleeds over into every aspect of our daily lives. It makes unsolved problems more profitable for politicians, bankers, and corporations. When the working class loses everything in a financial bust, we are more likely to surrender our constitutional rights in exchange for government assistance. Dependence is the key strategy within the Keynesian Kings' game of control.

Instead of serving people, the political financial class is focused on intentionally dividing people with entertainment and clownish controversies. This is a designed distraction. The goal is to hide their money printer while working people pay attention and pay taxes for a circus clown show.

Think about it. When any circus is broken, the ringleader sends out his clowns to distract the audience. What is different about this moment in history is that a growing few within the audience are refusing to be distracted. The audience now has a better option: An option to defund political corruption. An option to turn off the money printer. An option to peacefully separate money from the church of government.

Before we talk about this new option, you need to form an idea about what makes for a good money. In this book, we follow the general guidelines endorsed by free market economists. This framework is called the **6 Characteristics of Good Money**.[14]

6 Characteristics of Good Money:

1. Scarce: Limited supply in circulation, so that money retains its value.
2. Durable: Able to withstand wear and tear over time.
3. Portable: Easily transported, without being too heavy or bulky.

4. Acceptable: Easily identifiable to quickly verify authenticity and accept payment.
5. Divisible: Easily divided into smaller units, such as coins or bills of different denominations.
6. Uniform: All units are equal to one another and can be exchanged for goods and services.

Armed with this framework for good money, we can now explore why past money standards have failed. Taking a quick trip through monetary history will help you avoid repeating past money mistakes, so you will be prepared for money's future.

A TIMELINE OF FAILURES

Throughout history, our ancestors chose to outsource the work of creating new units of money to rare physical items.

If money is a tool to store the human energy expended while working to improve nature, it makes sense that money should respect the laws of nature. Money should be equally difficult for anyone on Earth to make more of. Regardless of intentions, failed money experiments like diluted Roman silver coins and fractional gold reserves in banks have proven that physical commodity-based systems are prone to human corruption.

Historic economies tried to peg the creation of new money units to nature. Mining for new money required hard work to expand the total money supply. If I wanted to steal from you, I had to steal through obvious means such as theft, counterfeiting, slave labor, or predatory taxation. Historical money was infused with the natural scarcity of Earth to protect the purchasing power of our ancestors' work across time.

Have you ever wondered why our ancestors chose money made by nature? I imagine they sat around a fire and asked the same question you and I are asking right now, "Who makes my money?" — and history shows our ancestors trusted natural money over human nature.

Here are seven insightful natural money experiments throughout history. Can you spot the common flaw?

1. **Cattle Standard**: Ancient Egyptians (5000 B.C. – 3100 B.C.) Cows, sheep, and goats were used as money. The animals were important to the people, yet cattle were not good money because animal lifespans were short, transportation was difficult, and cattle required a lot of care.[15]

2. **Grain Standard:** Ancient Mesopotamians (4000 B.C. – 539 B.C.)[16]
    Grains such as wheat, barley, and rice were vital to survival and therefore used as money to trade for other goods and services. Grains were not good money because of their perishable nature and the fluctuation in supply, which depended on weather conditions.

3. **Rai Stone Standard:** Yap Islanders in Micronesia (1000 A.D. – 1900 A.D.)[17]
    Rai stones were big circular disks made of limestone. These heavy stones were mined on a separate island and required a lot of work to bring back to Yap. Since the stones were difficult to move around, the islanders transferred ownership of the stones through verbal agreements. Some rai stones were lost at sea, yet they still counted as money as most of the tribe trusted that the stones still existed. In 1871, David Dean O'Keefe was shipwrecked on the island and introduced locals to iron tools; these made it easier to extract new rai stones and made them less valuable. Rarity and trust in ownership were lost and the use of rai stones as money ended.

4. **Seashell Standard:** Pacific Islanders (unknown – 1900 A.D.) Cowrie shells were valuable because they were rare, uniform, and beautiful. The overharvesting of new shells from their natural habitats lead to erratic supply. The unpredictable scarcity of shells opened the door for new types of money to be accepted. European traders introduced new money, like coins

and paper money, and islanders began using those types of money instead.

5. **Land Standard**: Medieval Europe (1000 A.D. – 1600 A.D.) Land ownership was a valuable resource that represented wealth and power, as land could be used to grow crops, raise cattle, and support a community. Land fails as money because it is not easily transferable, divisible, and it is fixed in place which makes it less useful for trade across distances. Land is also subject to extreme changes in value. Factors such as political instability, weather, or natural disasters made land an unreliable form of money. Feudalism failed and was replaced primarily with coinage.[18]

6. **Glass Bead Standard:** West Africans (1400 A.D. – 1900 A.D.) Glass beads were a rare good in West Africa, and were therefore used as money. When 14th-century European traders brought a lot of beads to Africa, these local beads became less valuable. Europeans traded their abundant supply of glass beads for more scarce things like gold and ivory. Over time, trust in the scarcity of beads was lost and European coins were adopted as better money.[19]

7. **Gold Standard:** Industrial America (1879 A.D. – 1971 A.D.) During the Industrial Revolution, American currency was backed by gold. Large stockpiles of existing gold prevented gold miners from quickly inflating the total money supply. This stabilized prices and encouraged economic growth. The main drawback of gold as money was difficulty to store it and its indivisibility in smaller transactions. Banks began to offer custody solutions as paper notes backed by gold deposits. To increase profits and offer "free" services, banks began to fractionally back their note issuance ("fractional reserve banking," or FRB). FRB allowed banks to lend more IOU notes than gold held in their vaults. Banks and governments could not quickly make more gold to cover waves of withdrawal requests. Custodied gold caused bank runs and crashes. Central

bankers concluded that gold was too difficult to manage, and a more flexible currency was needed to avoid bank runs.[20]

Did you spot the one common flaw? Different combinations of the 6 Characteristics of Good Money were broken within each monetary experiment, but trust was the common defect. Trust in the money was required for the system to work, and trust was ultimately broken.

These were the specific ways in which these failed money systems violated trust:

- Ancient Egyptians: Trusted supply of cattle would live long, healthy lives and their value would outweigh maintenance costs.
- Ancient Mesopotamians: Trusted supply of grain would continue to be replenished after each harvest.
- Yap Islanders: Trusted unseen rai stones existed, production of new units would remain difficult, and verbal ownership would continue to be enforceable.
- Pacific Islanders: Trusted supply of cowrie shells would continue to be harvested responsibly.
- Medieval Europeans: Trusted that politics, wars, and natural disasters would not devalue their land.
- West Africans: Trusted new glass beads would continue to be as difficult to create for Europeans as they were for West Africans.
- Industrial Americans: Trusted that banks would not lend out more gold-backed dollars than their withdrawable gold deposits.

When trust is broken, money systems collapse and are replaced by better money. How do you build trustworthy money? Transparency builds trust. History suggests money always gravitates towards the most trusted ledger, and the most trusted ledger is the most transparent ledger.

Therefore, logic says that transparency should be added as the 7th Characteristic of Good Money.

7 Characteristics of Good Money:

1. Scarce: Limited supply in circulation, so that money retains its value.
2. Durable: Able to withstand wear and tear over time.
3. Portable: Easily transported, without being too heavy or bulky.
4. Acceptable: Easily identifiable to quickly verify authenticity and accept payment.
5. Divisible: Easily divided into smaller units, such as coins or bills of different denominations.
6. Uniform: All units are equal to one another and can be exchanged for goods and services.
7. **Transparent: Ability of users to audit rules, ownership, and total money supply.**

You can now see how broken trust is the common flaw of past monetary systems. It is no coincidence that seven is known as the number of conclusions. From the story of creation in the book of Genesis to the days of the week on the Gregorian calendar, humanity may have found the conclusion to its many money experiments. Only if the rules of money are transparent to all can a monetary system be trusted. It's time to expose the debt-fueled monetary system. Backed only by trust in government, a new form of electronic paper debt was born: fiat money.

FIAT MONEY BASICS

"The United States can pay any debt it has because we can always print money to do that." —Alan Greenspan, *NBC News.*[21]

New units of fiat money are mined by the creation of debt.

This process of manufacturing fiat money is called "fractional reserve banking." In the FRB system, your bank is only required to keep a small fraction of reserves in deposits to issue new loans. Historically, cash reserve requirements for US banks have been 3-10% of loans outstanding. That means for every $100 you deposit into your bank account; the bank is required to keep between $3 and $10 available for withdrawal.

On March 15, 2020, the Board of the Federal Reserve reduced the US Reserve Requirement to 0%.[22]

In the fog of the pandemic, the private US banking sector was granted a license to create new money units without any deposits. Proponents for this policy point to the non-binding nature of this requirement as being superseded by bank safety regulations focused on liquidity. There is little benefit for us to dive into the regulatory weeds of Basel, HQLA, or LCR; we need only to look at the results.

M2 measures the nation's overall stash of cash, coins, bills, bank deposits, and money market funds, and is the official measurement for total money supply. From August of 2007 to August of 2022, the M2 money supply of the US dollar grew from $7.4 trillion to $21.6 trillion. Fifteen years of emergency excuses — from the great financial crisis of 2008 to the COVID-19 pandemic of 2020 — gave the Federal Reserve permission to increase the US dollar supply by 192%.[23] Call it inflation, devaluation, debasement, or quantitative easing — it doesn't matter. Printing new money without new work is theft.

Inflation is intentional. The Keynesian Kings fund their loans with inflation. Inflation is how government deficit spending and Wall Street asset purchases are financed. The slow transfer of wealth away from the working class has been like the subtle shift from twilight into nightfall.

How does this system of subtle theft remain solvent? To answer that question, we must lean into first-principles thinking and consider a banker's incentives. As the principle of any loan is paid off, the bank destroys those money units and keeps the interest as its profit.

Therefore, the banking industry maximizes profits by increasing interest payments. There is no financial incentive for lenders or borrowers to pay off loans and shrink the total money supply. The most profitable path for banks is to refinance loans and perpetually expand the money supply to maximize their interest payments. Borrowers are incentivized to refinance loans and perpetually expand the money supply to devalue the currency unit that backs their debt. This broken incentive structure shrinks the purchasing power of all fiat money over time.

The mutual incentive for banks and borrowers to constantly refinance debt explains why the world is drowning in debt. As of 2023, global debt is over $300 trillion dollars and growing. That's 349% of global GDP, or $37,500 of average debt per person, versus GDP per capita of $12,000 per person.[24]

Who benefits most from the status quo? Wall Street uses money supply expansion to maximize their profits through asset inflation and debt debasement. Banks use money supply expansion to maximize profits through open credit lines that pump their profits with perpetual interest payments. And politicians use money supply expansion to enable government overspending that buys votes without directly raising taxes.

How do you win as the value of money is melting? You win by being granted first access to cheap debt. This is called the Cantillon effect: Friends of the Keynesian Kings gain an advantage by receiving new money before the inflation caused by printing new money causes prices to go up.

The Cantillon effect explains why the richest in our society position themselves closest to the banks and politicians. If I run a big business with access to cheap debt, my small business competition doesn't stand a chance. Even worse, if I can use loans to print new money for campaign donations, then I can bribe my favorite politicians to write targeted regulations where only my company can afford to comply with the law.

Checkmate; profits on auto-pilot go to the fiat monopoly man!

Within a fiat-based economy, you will also notice more non-financial companies like department stores offering credit cards. On the surface, this appears to be a way to save on credit card fees and increase customer loyalty. Yes, those are minor benefits. But the bigger benefit is that these retail corporations get to become quasi-financial companies. This opens the pipelines of cheap money and floods out their competition.

Politicians on the left blame crony capitalism. Politicians on the right blame creeping communism. The truth is free markets cannot exist when the cost of money is not a free market. Central banks artificially set funding rates well below what savers would accept as interest rates in a free market. This is not the invisible hand of a free market; it is the invisible fist of market manipulation. As fiat money expands artificially in supply, debt creation is rewarded with dollar debasement and savings are punished with less purchasing power.

Currency debasement, also known as inflation, steals economic energy from the economy. It is legalized counterfeiting of your work. Currency devaluation is necessary for perpetual credit lines to exist, and it is allowed by our political system because it funds government overspending.

A barrage of fact bombs exploding in your mind about money can only be constructive for so long. Now is the perfect time to tell a story. Let's take a moment to grow our understanding of ethical money by harnessing the power of our imaginations.

ISLAND OF THE BOOK

Imagine you and I are on a ship together. We crash and swim toward a remote island with 98 other survivors. You and I are exhausted, yet thankful to be alive. Our ship sank in uncharted waters, so all survivors come to grips with the reality that there is no hope of rescue. We must start over and make this little tropical island our new home.

Island life is more difficult than it sounds. There is a lot of hard work to be done! We have an economics problem. We need a way to track the value we give to one another and the value we take from one another. We need a way to trade with each other: We need good money.

You and I listen as an alpha lawyer and cunning banker spar in a fiery debate over whether seashells or coconuts would make for better money. Then suddenly, a girl steps forward with a priceless possession. In her little hand she holds the scarcest item on our island, a book.

The lawyer is rendered speechless. "A book," the banker gasps!

After three months of searching our island, this little girl holds the only known book to survive our shipwreck. Our last written memory of the homeland we left behind, represented by 100 laminated pages of a children's story. Its personal significance to this little girl along with the waterproof nature of its laminated pages must have allowed it to survive our wet escape.

In a soft tone, this shy little girl begins to speak. "I know it is not much, but you can use my *Goldie Locks* book as money if you would like."

We all watch as the banker carefully tears each page from the spine of this little girl's book. A deep sadness overtakes many of the islanders, but the sweet-spirited little girl chimes in and says, "At least my most valuable possession is being shared among everyone."

Left with a stack of 100 laminated pages, the banker and lawyer proclaim, "Each page of this last surviving book will represent 1 unit of money on our island! Future generations will admire the generosity of this little girl and revere the genius behind the simplicity of starting our economy by sharing 100 units of money among 100 islanders. This little girl's gift will be remembered for generations to come!"

A doctor takes a pair of scissors from his first aid kit and hands them over to the banker. The banker cuts each page into 100 equal pieces. After finishing his cuts, he exclaims, "Now the trading of our 10,000 Goldie Locks can begin! Come and take your share! Let's get to work!"

Cooperation on our island quickly accelerates. Each of us looks for better ways to help our neighbors in exchange for a larger share of the 10,000 Goldie Locks. Innovation improves the value of products and services with every day that passes, so the price for the island's goods and services gets cheaper with time. We all expect real value in exchange for our share of the 10,000 Goldie Locks, so busy work is not rewarded.

You and I set goals regarding what percentage of the Goldie Locks we hope to own by the end of the year. "I want to own 10% of all the Goldie Locks by next year, how about you?" This metric of wealth is a common conversation among islanders. The incentive to work hard for a limited and transparent supply of 10,000 Goldie Locks has encouraged an explosion of innovation on our island!

There is one problem with our Goldie Locks system: Sometimes people misplace their money. Since our Goldie Locks become rarer with every square that is lost, mishandled money is considered a donation of purchasing power to everyone else's existing money. As good neighbors, we voluntarily help people who misplace their money with a type of unspoken insurance fund among trusted individuals and families.

The banker spots this lost money problem as an opportunity to help in his own way. Equipped with seasoned money security experience from his former profession, he designs an island bank to keep the islanders' Goldie Locks safe from theft, loss, and destruction. Business booms for his bank, but surprisingly prices on the island have not dropped in months. The lawyer, now our newly elected mayor, suggests that islanders have become lazy and must work harder to decrease prices again. The whole situation smells fishy.

As the banker closes up shop one evening, you and I decide to follow him. Under the cover of darkness, we watch as this elderly banker waddles toward an abandoned cave. Without any refrain, we hear the banker greet our newly elected major with a vulgar gesture before awkwardly shifting to business talk with a traditional handshake. At the same time, we both quietly ask one another, "What is going on?"

Without blowing our cover, we quietly creep closer toward the cave and settle into a hiding spot. Behind a large boulder, we borrow the flickering light of the two conspirators' torches to illuminate this forbidden meeting. We see the silhouettes of these two short and stoutly men standing beside what appears to be a pile of glass bottles, a stack of sticks, and a large barrel exuding a pungent fishy smell. The smell is intolerable. We both gag from 100 feet away! "What is going on?" I say again. Without a torch of our own, we decide to return at daylight.

At sunrise, we return to find the abandoned cave emptied of all supplies. Sadly, you and I think we will be forced into enduring another night of that fishy smell again. Then suddenly, I look down at your feet and notice something odd. The dark cave has gifted us with one tiny, overlooked piece of evidence: A small piece of parchment paper cut in the square shape of a Goldie Lock has attached itself to your left shoe.

You pick up the paper square to examine it further. "Where did they find paper? Why is this so sticky and smelly?" It feels like a million questions are flooding our minds at the same time. Only one question has a clear answer. What were the banker and mayor doing last night? They were counterfeiting our Goldie Locks. We have an obligation to compile evidence and let our neighbors know about this crime.

I share our evidence with my brother who works at the bank. He is shocked to see the counterfeit Goldie Locks we found. My brother eagerly agrees to join our investigation. While the banker is out for lunch, my brother quickly shuffles through the banker's records. What he finds is evidence as clear as a blue-sky day. In his hands he holds a complete record of every counterfeit Goldie Lock ever created, and accompanied by receipts from a fisherman, lumberjack, and lifeguard.

Over the last year, the banker has doubled the number of Goldie Locks on our island! That means I have to earn twice as many Goldie Locks to hit my goal of owning 10% of the Goldie Locks by next year! And who knows how many I would have to earn to keep up with his counterfeiting operation. It is time to confront the banker and the new mayor in front of the entire island. We call a tribal council!

You, my brother, and I lay out the evidence of this counterfeiting operation as clear as the fishy smell on Hippy Bob's breath after last year's rationed "all-coconut" week during the construction of our angling equipment. Our case is so tight that our banker and mayor do not even try to deny their counterfeiting crimes. Instead, they begin to justify them.

The banker argues, "I have more demand for loans than I have supply of Goldie Locks in my deposits. To meet demand, I have to create more Goldie Locks. In fact, our system of creating more Goldie Locks with octopus' ink, paper from messages in washed-up bottles, and laminate from tree sap is the only way we can meet demand for my requested loans. An elastic money supply is needed for loans to grow our economy."

The mayor argues, "I promised to create more jobs. Without giving our banker the ability to create more loans, then islanders cannot get access to the Goldie Locks they need to expand their businesses and hire more people. If you want your paycheck and businesses to grow, then allow us to create more Goldie Locks. Otherwise, decreasing prices will destroy the incentive for people to work hard on our island."

After many years of silence, the same shy little girl who donated her *Goldie Locks* book stepped forward. In the midst of the economic chaos caused by the counterfeiting operation, we know the crowd will hang on whatever words she would share with us. The crowd grows silent. In an attempt to restore order on our island, this now young woman slowly shares three simple, and yet profoundly wise words.

"Counterfeiting is theft."

In unison, the islanders agree with a "yes, it is!" as she steps back into the crowd. Our island judge summons a jury for sentencing.

The doctor makes the case to hang them both. I suggest they both be banished from our island; I want to give them 30 days to build a boat and gather supplies before being sent on their way.

Just before sentencing, the judge asks the young woman with the book for her opinion on sentencing. In a gentle voice, she says, "I memorized every page from the book I loved and donated as a little girl. My memory can help remove every counterfeit Goldie Lock from the island's money supply. I trust my neighbors who were stolen from by counterfeit money will be helped by other neighbors who held the real Goldie Locks. I suggest the banker and lawyer be required by law to work and restore the accounts of all the islanders who were given fake Goldie Locks. Once all of their debts are repaid, they should get a second chance on this island."

After a few years of helping their neighbors and selling their possessions acquired with fake Goldie Locks, the banker and former mayor repaid all of the people who held counterfeit Goldie Locks with real Goldie Locks. People on the island of the book lived prosperously ever after.

—

Simple money is better money. There was a time when money was a much simpler tool than the political currency units most of us use today. Before looking forward, we must look back at how the Keynesian Kings were granted the right to counterfeit money, so it never happens again.

THE AMERICAN GOLDEN AGE

The best way to rob a bank is to own one. —William K. Black, Senior VP Federal Home Loan Bank of San Francisco.[25]

The US Coinage Act of 1879 fixed the value of gold coins at $20.67 per ounce.

This simple money standard resulted in decades of stable prices. From 1880 through 1914, the annual inflation rate averaged just 0.1% in the United States.[26] Hard dollars liberated a generation to focus on solving hard problems. Armed with a stable currency, investors funded inventors who hired workers to build more technological breakthroughs than any previous generation in human history. During this period of gold-backed money, the world was introduced to electric lighting, automobiles, airplanes, radios, and landline telephones.[27]

Fiat-funded economists will criticize this period for excessive income inequality. However, the US Census Bureau data shows the top

1% of US households controlled under 15% of total national income in the 1890s compared to almost 20% in the 2010s.[28] Under progressive monetary policy and debt-laden entitlement programs, income inequality has gotten worse, not better.

Fiat-funded academia paints cartoonish characterizations of 19th-century capitalists like John D. Rockefeller and Andrew Carnegie as greedy, mustached monopoly men who stole labor from the working class, but the real story is much more nuanced. These businessmen were aggressive, but both advanced our modern world with productive products and neither siphoned off as much labor from the working class as what came next. By the turn of the 20th century, the greed of men would slow the speed of technological advancement to a grinding halt.

BIRTH OF THE FEDERAL RESERVE

Despite the Coinage Act of 1879, US banks failed to hold adequate gold reserves to cover their credit lines. The Panic of 1907 plunged the American banking sector into a liquidity crisis. Working people went to withdraw money from the bank, but it wasn't there.[29] Six years later, the Federal Reserve Act was passed on December 23, 1913. This delayed response to the Panic of 1907 crisis established a network of private banks to control the price of money.

The term "private bank" is an agreed-upon lie and a façade. From the beginning, this network of too-big-to-fail banks was designed to be a government-supported monopoly to extract rent from the total sum of financial activity that occurs within the US economy.

Did you know the Federal Reserve expanded the money supply by 63.4% in the 1920s while the US gold reserves expanded by only 15%?[30]

Despite being officially on a gold standard, US banks were permitted by the Federal Reserve to create four times more money than the growth of its gold reserves. This credit expansion within the fractional reserve banking system happened mostly by growing money substitutes, such as credit union shares, time deposits, and life insurance cash surrender liabilities without gold-backing. Austrian economist Murray N. Rothbard, points to this unnatural increase in money supply beyond gold reserves as the root cause of malinvestment that led to the Great Depression.

While easy money fueled speculation on Wall Street, main street lost faith in the backing of gold to dollars in their bank accounts. Whispers of bank insolvencies swept the land, and their suspicions were justified. Banks were overleveraged and could not print more gold to cover their customers' deposits. When customers went to withdraw gold, it wasn't there. Thousands of families lost their entire life savings overnight.

Between 1930 and 1933, about 9,000 banks failed and lost almost $30 billion worth of deposits (in 2023 dollars) — 4,000 banks failed in 1933 alone, driven by bank runs based on widespread rumors that newly elected President Franklin D. Roosevelt would ban gold ownership.[31] The Federal Reserve tried to restore confidence in the banking sector by raising interest rates on deposits to 1920 levels, but it was too late.[32] Everything crashed. New measures were needed to restore trust in the US dollar.

THE NEW STEAL

No such banking institution or branch shall pay out, export, earmark, or permit the withdrawal or transfer in any manner or by any device whatsoever, of any gold or silver coin or bullion or currency or take any other action which might facilitate the hoarding thereof; nor shall any such banking institution or branch pay out deposits, make loans or discounts, deal in foreign exchange, transfer credits from the United States to any place abroad, or transact any other banking business whatsoever.[33] —President Franklin D. Roosevelt, Proclamation 203, March 6, 1933.

Just 36 hours after his inauguration, President Franklin D. Roosevelt proclaimed a bank holiday in response to widespread bank runs and the threat of a financial crisis during the Great Depression. Americans would not have access to their bank accounts for an entire week, during which time the federal government would assess the financial health of each bank.

If your bank was deemed insolvent by the government, it was forced to close or consolidate with another bank. If your bank received the government's seal of approval, then it was allowed to reopen with new privileges. The Emergency Banking Act was passed only a few days later. FDR bragged this new legislation was passed "promptly and patriotically" by Congress.

Title IV of The Emergency Banking Act gave 12 Federal Reserve banks a new privilege. Now these banks would have the privilege of issuing emergency currency in the form of Federal Reserve Bank Notes that could be backed by any assets belonging to a commercial bank. No longer were banks constrained by the gold standard. This legislation would fundamentally reshape the US banking system even though many leaders in Congress complained they were not given adequate time to read the legislation before a vote was called.[34]

> *"I can assure you that it is safer to keep your money in a reopened bank than under the mattress."*[35] —President Franklin D. Roosevelt in his first Fireside Chat, March 12, 1933

Twenty-four days after his first Fireside Chat, FDR outlawed private gold ownership with Executive Order 6102.

Three-hundred days after ordering people to surrender their gold to the government, FDR signed the Gold Reserve Act of 1934. This legislation devalued the US dollar from $20.67 per gold ounce to $35.00 per gold ounce.

This meant 41% more dollars were required to buy the same one ounce of gold. People who took financial advice from their president had their gold purchasing power devalued by 41% in less than one year.

If your great-grandfather took his president's advice and traded his 16 ounces of gold savings for US dollars, you would inherit $330 in 2023. If your great-grandfather kept his 16 ounces of gold under his mattress, you inherited $31,616 in 2023. The FDR-approved banks were not safe.

It wasn't until December 31, 1974, that the US officially lifted the 41-year ban on private ownership of gold coins, bullion, and certificates. This unconstitutional law gave the fiat banking sector time to rebuild and solidify the infrastructure for an entirely credit-based money system.[36]

Amid the fog of bank runs, the Banking Act was signed by FDR on June 16, 1933. Often referred to as the Glass-Steagall Act, this law established the Federal Deposit Insurance Corporation. The FDIC was chartered to serve as an independent federal agency to maintain stability and public confidence in the financial system. This insurance aimed to restore confidence in the security of deposits in US banks among the working class.

As of September 30, 2022, the FDIC held $125.5 billion dollars of reserves to cover $9.926 trillion dollars' worth of deposits, a mere 1.26% reserve ratio.[37] The real FDIC insurance is the Federal Reserve's promise to print dollars when any FDIC-insured bank becomes insolvent due to overextended risk. The 2008 great financial crisis showed the true colors of FDIC insurance: privatized gains and socialized losses.

In 2008, the idea of "too big to fail" was broadcasted by bankers and politicians. The working class was too busy to ask how we got there.

The highway to hell is paved with good intentions. From 2000 to 2007, the Keynesian Kings flooded the US real estate market with cheap new money to gamble on risky investments like subprime mortgage-backed securities. Politicians operated under the moral guise of expanding home ownership; banks operated under the protection of FDIC-insured bank deposits. This was mutually assured financial destruction.

The Federal Reserve became concerned about the dollar quickly losing value against real estate, so this board of seven presidentially appointed central bankers decided to return interest rates to pre-9/11 levels. The house of cards collapsed when rates were raised up to 5.25% in 2007.[38] After making obscene profits on the way up, the Keynesian Kings demanded to be rescued by bailouts on the way down and American politicians were held hostage to the possibility of widespread failure of FDIC-insured bank deposits.

Instead of letting bad banks fail, American politicians granted banks more power to print money in exchange for accepting more regulations.

On the surface, more regulation of the banking industry sounds like a good thing. However, self-written regulations only strengthened the unholy alliance between banks and government. Banks would write blank checks for government overspending and the government would write fill-in-the-blank legislation to protect big banks from competition.

When money is free to print, only trust is required for the money to remain solvent.

How did the Keynesian Kings amass the power to print money that is trusted by the rest of the world?

Let's take one final step backward to understand the Keynesian Kings' path to global money-printing power.

PATH TO PRINTING POWER

In the summer of 1944, representatives from 44 nations came together in Bretton Woods, New Hampshire. Their mission was to create a new international monetary system. After the devastation of World War II, the goal of the conference was to establish a framework for economic cooperation between countries. The historical ramifications of this seemingly benign conference cannot be overstated.

The Bretton Woods conference established the International Monetary Fund and most importantly it laid the foundation for a fixed exchange rate system, which pegged US dollars to gold and other major currencies to the US dollar.

Harry Dexter White and John Maynard Keynes at Bretton Woods, July 1944.[39]

The US delegation was led by **Harry Dexter White, Assistant Secretary of the Treasury.**

"Russia is the first instance of a socialist economy in action … and it works!"[40] —Harry Dexter White, Assistant Secretary of the Treasury

FBI Director, J. Edgar Hoover, submitted a report to US President Harry Truman with evidence that Harry Dexter White was a Soviet spy. Truman immediately rescinded White's nomination as managing director of the IMF. As to not upset the Bretton Woods agreement which gave America the right to issue the world's reserve currency, Truman excused the recension of Harry Dexter White saying, "It would not be proper to have Americans as the heads of both bodies."[41]

The British delegation was led by the British economist **John Maynard Keynes.**

"Lenin was certainly right. There is no subtler, no surer means of overturning the existing basis of society than to debauch the currency. The process engages all the hidden forces of economic law on the side of destruction and does it in a manner which not one man in a million is able to diagnose."[42] —John Maynard Keynes, *The Economic Consequences of the Peace.*

Beyond the moral failings of Keynes, it is worth noting that Keynes once described his views as extremely left of Fabian Socialist co-founder Sidney Webb. Keynes lacked the progressive patience of Webb to slowly move the world toward socialism.[43] It is quite ironic that the two individuals most responsible for the postwar monetary system publicly favored communism over capitalism.

At Bretton Woods, White and Keynes sparred between a global dollar or bancor system, but ultimately they walked away with an agreement that convinced most of the world to store their nation's gold in the United States and peg their currencies to the gold-backed US dollar. America boomed after World War II, in large part due to its new status as the official world reserve currency.

Twenty-seven years later, the entire Bretton Woods system collapsed. Once again, bankers and politicians fell for the monetary temptation to print money without work. America abused its gold reserves and used the secrecy of Fort Knox to create new US dollars to spend beyond their gold reserves. International rumors of US insolvency were beginning to spread and new measures were needed to rebuild trust in the dollar.

1971 GOLDEN DEFAULT

Facing inflationary pressure, the Coinage Act of 1965 authorized the removal of silver from dimes and quarters. The replacement base metal was changed from scarce silver to an abundant copper-nickel alloy. Following in the footsteps of the Roman Denarius, the 1965 coin dilution coincided with extreme government expansion after US

President Lyndon B. Johnson enacted the Great Society program and escalated the Vietnam War.

In the late 1960s, the United States was running large budget deficits which concerned foreign governments and central banks. Fearing the peg between gold and the US dollar was becoming unstable, there was a bank run on gold reserves at Fort Knox as foreign entities increasingly requested gold for dollars. To address this problem, US President Richard Nixon announced on August 15, 1971, that the United States would temporarily suspend the conversion of US dollars to gold at a fixed value, effectively ending the gold standard agreement of Bretton Woods.

After more than 50 years, that temporary suspension of the gold standard still remains. What is more interesting is what came next. America did something no other empire had ever accomplished in human history. It transformed its national debt from a liability into the reserve asset of the world. In Chapter 3, we discuss how the "black gold" standard established US government debt (Treasury bonds) as the reserve asset of the world; the rest is history.

To summarize, Nixon's unprecedented move allowed the US government to print new dollars without having to worry about backing new units with new gold reserves. Unofficially, this was a debt default, and the immediate impact was double-digit inflation in the 1970s. Nixon's Bretton Woods default caused massive dollar devaluation which bled the 1970s economy. New measures were needed to restore trust in the dollar.

Paul Volcker was appointed chairman of the Federal Reserve in August of 1979 to implement a tight monetary policy to rein in inflation. Volcker raised the interest rates above inflation rates which allowed the supply gains from new technology to catch up with the increased supply of dollars printed for LBJ's Great Society. Though unpopular with financial markets at the time, Volcker was laser-focused on rebuilding trust in the dollar. He increased the price of printing new dollars by raising the federal discount rate up to 18% in May of 1981.[44] By creating a high interest rate environment, Volcker tamed inflation, but skyrocketed the average 30-year fixed rate mortgage up to 18.6%.[45]

What was different in 1981 than today is the size of the US national debt. In 1981, the United States carried a federal debt of $964.5 million dollars compared to over $32.6 trillion dollars in 2023. If rates were to rise to the level of Volcker, the federal interest expense on the US national debt would be over $6 trillion dollars per year. Considering that the US federal government spent $6.27 trillion[46] total in 2022, the reality of spending $6 trillion on interest payments is unrealistic. The 1981 inflation playbook is out of date; a new solution must be considered.

Before we can explore new solutions to save the United States from a painful debt spiral, we must first put the nail in the coffin of fiat money by understanding how it has been used for bailouts and why bailouts have been devastating to the working class.

TOO BIG TO FAIL

"I've abandoned free market principles to save the free market system."[47]— US President George W. Bush, December 16, 2008, CNN State of the Union with Candy Crowley.

What is a bailout?

Without diving too deep into the technical details of TARP or Quantitative Easing, the most important takeaway from the 2008 great financial crisis is the ethical crisis of bailouts. In this centrally planned, quasi-socialist system, profits are privatized while losses are socialized. The Keynesian Kings placed a bet that taxpayers would bail out their financial gambling under the slogan of "too big to fail" — and they won the bet.

Who benefited from the 2008 great financial crisis? From 2001 to 2007, Washington, D.C., politicians got to raise campaign funds on the platform of "affordable home ownership for all" and Wall Street used cheap money to gamble on subprime mortgage-backed securities.

In layman's terms, bailout means the US Treasury spent new money like a drunken sailor, but in respect of drunken sailors, at least they spend their own money. The American surrender to socialism culminated in a full-fledged central bank shopping spree during the COVID-19 pandemic.

The Federal Reserve balance sheet grew by over ten times from $865 billion in June of 2007 to $8.9 trillion dollars in June of 2022.[48] With a few keystrokes, this group of bankers and bureaucrats printed trillions of new dollars to buy government debt, private equities, and mortgage-backed securities.[49] Instead of allowing the arsonists who set the financial system on fire to go bankrupt, a bailout precedent was set. With every crisis, the arsonists are hired as firefighters to spray fire hoses of fiat money and print away the prosperity of the working class.

From August of 2007 to August of 2022, Keynesian Kings nearly tripled the total dollar supply from $7.39 trillion to $21.63 trillion.[50] Basic economics says if you triple the supply of something then you must triple its demand or it is quickly going to lose value. Fabian Socialists desired a gradual bleeding of the capitalist economy, so a tripling of prices is unacceptable for the Keynesian Kings. Again, more extreme measures would need to be taken to increase the global demand for dollars to match the growing supply of dollars. How do the Keynesian Kings increase the demand for holding dollars? If history is written by the victors of war, it appears the losing nation's monetary policy is as well.

FINANCIAL VIOLENCE

How can a nation increase demand for its printed money?

1. Nation fights a war.
2. Nation wins a war.
3. Nation issues a loan to the losing nation in debt denominated in its printable money.

The winning nation gets to print new money without work to pay its debts while the losing nation must do real work to pay for its debts.

The International Monetary Fund carries out most of the dirty work to boost global demand for the dollar. Of the 190 countries with IMF membership, the United States accounts for the largest share of IMF funding at 17.46% of the total membership quota.

Remember, the IMF was spawned from the imaginations of Keynes and White at the 1944 Bretton Woods conference. After Nixon defaulted on the Bretton Woods gold standard of fixed exchange rates in 1971, the IMF conveniently broadened its mandate.

In 1975, the IMF "transformed itself from being an organization focused exclusively on issues of foreign exchange convertibility and global monetary stability to an organization having a much broader mandate: lending for a range of financial crisis, including debt, currency, and banking crises, and engaging in a wide range of issues including capital flows, financial regulations, and surveillance of the global economy."[51]

This broadened IMF mandate is responsible for much of the perpetual poverty we see around the world today. For the first time in human history, the debt of one nation is the global reserve currency of all other nations. All must work for it, but only the Keynesian Kings can print it.

As with every loan program, the devil is in the details. As of 2022, Argentina, Egypt, Ukraine, Pakistan, and Ecuador are the largest borrowers from the IMF. In exchange for refinancing loans that can never be paid back, poor nations agree to harsh structural readjustment terms.

Are poor countries exploited by IMF loans? Yes. These restructuring terms benefit rich IMF nation-state members. Predatory terms like local currency devaluation (strengthen US dollar), wage ceilings (cheap labor), exports of monocrops (coffee, tea, textiles, etc.), imports of food (grain, beef, chicken), and contracting foreign IMF nation-state companies to build infrastructure are a few ways poor countries are exploited.

IMF loans enrich multinational corporations and empower dictators who spend the funds on themselves with no intention of paying off the loan balances that are due 20-30 years in the future. If you'd like to learn more about the details of this broken system, I suggest you start by reading *Hidden Oppression: How the IMF and World Bank Sell Exploitation as Development* by Alex Gladstein of the Human Rights Foundation.[52] His book gives specific examples of IMF exploitation.

In summary, IMF loans require the flexibility of fiat money for their exploitation of weaker countries. Since fiat money is nothing more than debt backed by governments, it needs war, crisis, and more debt to maintain demand. Without new global demand for dollars, printing new supply of money quickly drives up prices and lowers living standards in the homeland of the money printer.

The American working class is finally feeling the pain necessary to pull back the curtain and see the Wizard of Oz who prints their money. The Keynesian Kings can afford to print away the value of fiat money, but the one thing they cannot afford to lose is working-class trust in fiat money. Time, mathematics, and ethics are not on their side.

THE FUTURE OF FIAT MONEY

What happens when working people learn their money is designed to steal from them?

The ancient dream of alchemy hinges on the idea that you keep your alchemy process a secret. If the public figures out you can transform abundant materials into rare gold, then gold will lose its value and your game is up. Sunlight is how we destroy this unholy art of fiat alchemy.

Like alchemy, fiat money is an unholy idea rooted in greed, sloth, and a desire to control the fruits of another man's labor. Under the current monetary system, rather than total money supply being restrained by the hard work required to extract gold, silver, or electricity, the only supply constraint on fiat money is the trust of the working-class people who trade their limited time for the unlimited electronic money.

There is that pesky flaw of trust popping up again. What happens when the working class no longer trusts fiat money?

Hyperinflation. When mass awareness of fake money hits main street, businesses and workers will no longer accept fake money for their real goods and services. People will demand to be paid in real money. Remember the good money framework we studied earlier in this chapter?

This time around, let's fill in this framework with characteristics of the dollar.

7 Characteristics of dollars as money:

1. Scarce: Growth in total supply means the dollar loses its value over time.
2. Durable: Digital cash is easily seized, and physical cash is unable to withstand wear and tear over time.
3. Portable: International transactions with dollars are costly, slow, and require political permission.
4. Acceptable: Counterfeit physical cash is difficult to spot in peer-to-peer transactions.
5. Divisible: Metal coinage is not divisible, digital, and is inconvenient to carry in day-to-day commerce.
6. Uniform: Unpredictable total supply makes dollars unequal across time which creates volatile prices.
7. Transparent: Ability of users to audit the rules, ownership, and total supply of US dollars does not exist.

When bad money fails, history says the economy will naturally reset into the money that checks the most boxes of the 7 Characteristics of Good Money framework. As you can see from above, the dollar is on borrowed time; it is wise to prepare for a great reset.

You don't have to panic buy into the next system of money. One day, many fiat money workers will wake up to find a majority of their life savings are worthless. As a good neighbor, you must be prepared and ready to help them when the fiat money Ponzi scheme falls apart.

How much longer do Americans have before hyperinflation crashes the dollar?

It is impossible to predict human psychology, so it is impossible to know when trust in the dollar will ultimately break.

The shift to better money will likely involve a mix of political censorship, sovereign defaults, and an explosion of interest payments on US national debt that spirals out of control. The socialist monopoly money will end, and a new era of better money will be ushered into existence.

To my surprise, I found the US Treasury Department released a grim forecast of US national debt as a percentage of GDP:

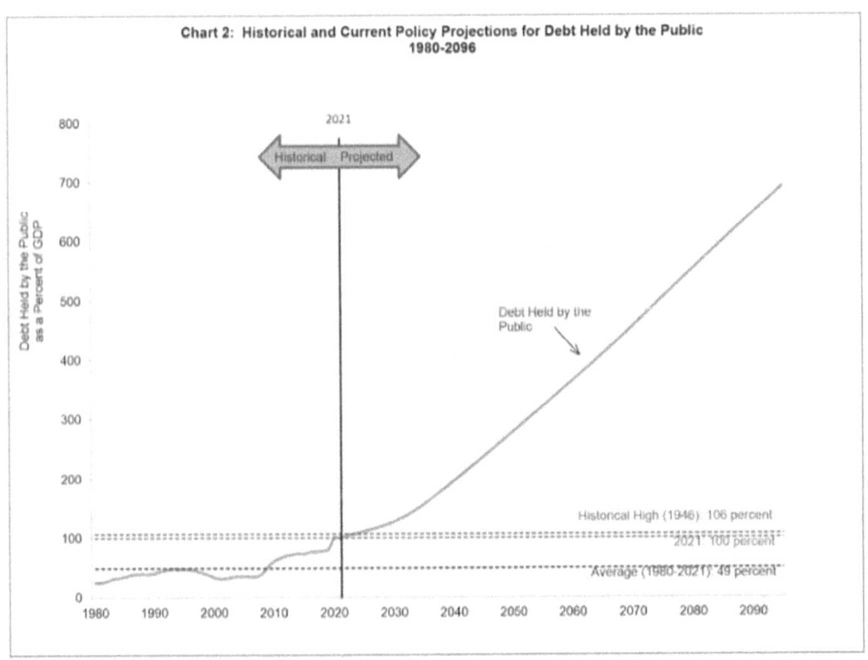

Source: US Treasury, "An Unsustainable Fiscal Path."[53]

The US government owes over $206 trillion in funded and unfunded debt liabilities. Individual debt liability per US citizen is $573,702, as of July 2023. That's a debt burden of over 15 times US median income and it's growing every day.[54]

United States private and public debts are spiraling out of control. The Keynesian Kings have divorced money creation from any real-world constraints. Keynesian economics has become a monetary system 100% based on public trust and 0% based on public verification. New dollar mining does not require equal amounts of work. To print new dollars, you must be granted political permission through citizenship, credit score, and state compliance.

The dollar is debt disguised as money. Debt is bondage. Global debt skyrocketed past $300 trillion in 2023.[55] At a debt ratio of over three times global GDP,[56] it is no surprise that the spiritual bondage of fear, greed, and hopelessness are sweeping across the world.

Remember Bretton Woods. In hindsight, two communist sympathizers successfully designed a global dollar-based monetary system that destroyed American capitalism from within. It is like Keynes and White knew that, slowly and gradually, the American people would default away from the gold standard and onto a purely debt-based system.

Most Americans have no idea what debt money is doing to their country and the rest of the world. This is by design. The unlimited dollar supply has progressively destroyed American capitalism with unlimited debt, unlimited corruption, and unlimited wars.

Bottom line, the dollar gives Americans an unfair monetary advantage. Being close to the money printer transfers the pain of hyperinflation onto poor countries who save in dollars without the accompanying government welfare benefits. For now, the United States is the only nation that can print away all its debts at the expense of poor countries whose debts are denominated in the currency of the United States. In America, debt is an asset. In poor countries, debt is a liability. If you support centrally planned money, how can you call yourself a free market capitalist?

Exporting inflation onto the world through the printing of dollars has created global relationships of subjugation instead of cooperation, which has instigated numerous wars. There are really no costs to anything the US government decides to do. War is profitable because new demand is created for the winning nation's currency.

A centrally planned money system means politicians can fight unlimited wars, politicians can continue to grow entitlements in exchange for votes, politicians can spend on anything, and they don't have to make hard decisions about what we prioritize as a nation.

I love the idea of America: A limited government established to protect life, liberty, and the pursuit of happiness. A political system decentralized across 50 states with a constitution to protect the rights of the smallest minority group — the individual. If democracy is two wolves and a lamb voting on what to eat for dinner, then liberty is a well-armed lamb contesting the vote.

As a lamb well-armed with the truth about fiat money, you are now ready to see why bitcoin is more American than the socialist dollar.

BITCOIN IS BETTER MONEY

Now that you have seen bad money, you are ready to see bitcoin as better money.

In a fiat-funded world, corporate media has tried to convince you that Bitcoin is too complex and risky for the average man. Fiat televangelists preach that cryptocurrency is just a fad that is used by drug dealers, terrorists, hackers, and tax evaders to circumvent the United States judicial system. Despite being the best-performing asset in human history, critics say bitcoin does not solve any real problems.

Crypto is the Keynesian Kings' favorite attack on Bitcoin. Warren Buffet, Charlie Munger, Bill Gates, and Jamie Dimon conflate frauds like Luna, Celsius, BlockFi, and FTX with bitcoin. The truth is, bitcoin does not compete with cryptocurrencies. Nearly all of the 20,000+ altcoins have founders and marketing teams who print crypto tokens without work. The crypto industry is mostly scammers selling shares in their software companies without proper SEC disclosures. In the property chapter, we'll discuss the fraud of altcoins.

For now, you should know that no other altcoin can compete with bitcoin as a global base layer money. The paychecks of the most outspoken Bitcoin critics rely on not understanding this simple fact. Mass ignorance intentionally delays Bitcoin adoption and profits the money printers.

There is no substitute for doing your own homework on something as important as Bitcoin. The money you choose to use, save, and trade for your finite time and talents is worthy of developing a basic understanding of how it works.

How difficult is it to use Bitcoin? If you can use an email, you can learn to use Bitcoin; Bitcoin technology is simple. The rules of Bitcoin are simple. The most difficult part of Bitcoin is seeing past the fiat propaganda and dropping the socialism strings attached to the dollars in your bank account. If you have made it this far into this chapter, you are ready for the truth.

To begin, let's revisit our good money framework once again. This time around, let's fill it in with Bitcoin characteristics.

7 Characteristics of Bitcoin as Money:

1. Scarce: Total supply of less than 21 million, so bitcoin appreciates in value over time.
2. Durable: Digital decentralized ownership of private keys makes bitcoin immune to physical wear and tear.
3. Portable: It is easy to transport bitcoin across borders with a 12- or 24-word recovery seed phrase.
4. Acceptable: Automatic authentication by signing devices prevents counterfeit transactions.
5. Divisible: 100 million units per bitcoin makes it usable for microtransactions.
6. Uniform: Equal units can be cheaply exchanged for goods in seconds over layer 2 protocols like the Lightning payment network.

7. Transparent: Public software code gives all users the ability to audit the rules, ownership, and total money supply.

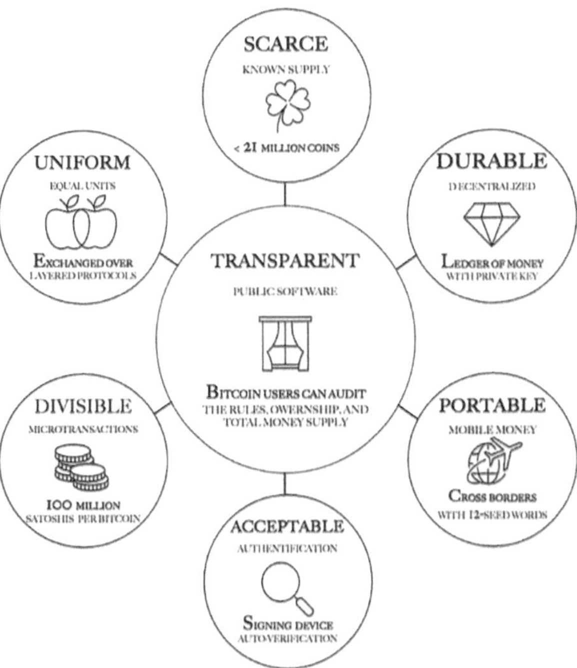

Bitcoin is better technology for money. If you hear politicians say they can fix our broken nation without mentioning our broken money, now you will know better. The Keynesian Kings are trying to sell expensive spackling to "fix" cracks in our nation's walls, but you have now seen the problem with our monetary foundation. It is impossible to make our country better without better money.

WHAT IS BITCOIN?

Bitcoin is an idea of what money should be. Since David Chaum's failed DigiCash in 1989, there have been almost one hundred other failed attempts at decentralized money.

BITCOIN PRE-HISTORY
95 FAILED DIGITAL CURRENCIES

ACC	CyberCents	IKP	MPTP	Proton
Agora	CyberCoin	IMB-MP	Net900	Redi-Charge
AIMP	CyberGold	InterCoin	NetBill	S/PAY
Allopass	DigiGold	Ipin	NetCard	Sandia Lab E-Cash
b-money	Digital Silk Road	Javien	NetCash	Secure Courier
BankNet	e-Comm	Karma	NetCheque	Semopo
Bitbit	E-Gold	LotteryTickets	NetFare	SET
Bitgold	Ecash	Lucre	No3rd	SET2Go
Bitpass	eCharge	MagicMoney	One Click Charge	SubScrip
C-SET	eCoin	Mandate	PayMe	Trivnet
CAFÉ	Edd	MicroMint	PayNet	TUB
Checkfree	eVend	Micromoney	PayPal	Twitpay
ClickandBuy	First Virtual	MilliCent	PaySafeCard	VeriFone
ClickShare	FSTC Electronic Check	Mini-Pay	PayTrust	VisaCash
CommerceNet	Geldkarte	Minitix	PayWord	Wallie
CommercePOINT	Globe Left	MobileMoney	Peppercoin	Way2Pay
CommerceSTAGE	Hashcash	Mojo	PhoneTicks	WorldPay
Cybank	HINDE	Mollie	Playspan	X-Pay
CyberCash	iBill	Mondex	Polling	

This point is profound. Bitcoin is not the first attempt at decentralized money; it is the first attempt at decentralized money *that worked.*[57]

The protocol was first released as a public software on January 3, 2009, by an undercover coder named Satoshi Nakamoto. Over a decade later, the Bitcoin software remains public for all to see and is downloaded on tens of thousands of cheap computers ("nodes") spread across the world. This army of nodes enforces the rules of Bitcoin and stores a record of all Bitcoin transactions that have ever occurred.

Bitcoin is a decentralized ledger. You cannot hold, touch, or see a bitcoin. When you own bitcoin, you own a private key that gives you control to sign a transaction that moves your bitcoin to another public address on the decentralized ledger.

You cannot store your bitcoin on a hardware wallet, USB stick, or a mobile app; a public address on the ledger, like an email address, stores your bitcoin. You use a wallet (signing device) to store *your private key* — like a password. Your private key allows you to broadcast signed transactions that send bitcoin from your public address to another public address.

It is by design that bitcoin is not stored on a wallet. Ownership is decentralized. Bitcoin is a common ledger, like a shared spreadsheet, where all Bitcoin transactions are stored on all the Bitcoin nodes spread across the world. If your signing device is lost or stolen, you can input a 12- or 24-word recovery seed phrase into any brand of Bitcoin signing device to restore access to your Bitcoin private key. Warning, if anyone gets hold of your 12- or 24-word recovery seed phrase, then they can send your bitcoin to a public address that you do not control.

WHAT IS BITCOIN MINING?

Once every ten minutes or so, a bitcoin mining computer guesses a random number called a nonce. The reward for the work — electricity/computing power — to find this nonce is called a block reward. The winning bitcoin miner receives a block subsidy, transaction fees, and the privilege of adding a new block of signed transactions to the Bitcoin ledger.

The block reward is reduced on a predictable schedule that releases 50% less bitcoin every 210,000 blocks, which occurs roughly every four years. This halving cycle of new bitcoin supply on a predictable schedule is how we know there will never be more than 21 million bitcoin in existence.

Bitcoin is the most secure computer network in human history. As of 2023, this Bitcoin network is guarded by over 275 TWh of encrypted energy and 430 EH/s of computing power.[58] These numbers mean nothing without real-world context, so let's take a shot at it.

275 TWh of encrypted energy is equivalent to about 48% of the total energy used by the gold mining industry.[59] Hash power of 430 EH/s is a representation of the network's computing power. This metric means bitcoin miners are making 430 quintillion guesses per

second to try to guess the nonce and win the block reward. How long would it take you to count to 430 quintillion? 138 trillion years.

The proof-of-work consensus protocol of the bitcoin mining network makes attacks against the protocol extremely foolish and expensive. If a bad actor tries to mine a block with invalid Bitcoin transactions, an army of cheap nodes will reject the bad block to protect the value of their bitcoin. The attacker is free to continue their fake Bitcoin blockchain, but it will be a lonely network and eventually a worthless version of a lie.

WHAT BACKS BITCOIN?

The US Securities and Exchange Commission (SEC) and Commodities Futures Trading Commission (CFTC) have publicly stated many times that bitcoin is a commodity.[60] Bitcoin is an asset without an issuer.

Only assets with issuers require something to back them up. The question of "What backs Bitcoin?" is thought pollution which has spilled over from the counterparty risk of fiat money. This critique is like asking what backs corn, wheat, oil, land, gold, or silver? Commodities do not need to be backed by anything. The physical work that brings commodities into usable existence is expended up front during their creation.

Unlike fiat money, shares of stock, or crypto tokens, it is equally difficult to create new units of bitcoin for everyone.

Bitcoin is a commodity money supported by three free market pillars:

1. User Ideology: Nodes download the Bitcoin rules and will not upgrade to a new software that violates their interests.
2. Physical Scarcity: Scarcity of mining computers and electricity raises the cost to mine an invalid block that will ultimately be rejected by nodes.

3. Public Transparency: Anyone can audit the public codebase of Bitcoin to look for bugs, backdoors, or weak points.

CONCLUSION

From the exodus of Moses to Jesus flipping over the tables of money changers, we can see the spiritual importance of allowing men to keep and voluntarily share the fruits of their labor. From the emancipation proclamation of Abraham Lincoln to Martin Luther King Jr.'s dream, we can see the moral importance of equal justice for all. Intentional inflation is predatory taxation and the antithesis of equal justice for all.

If you only take away one idea from this chapter, let it be this: Money should not steal from you. If it does, then it is your God-given right to use better money. Let's go one step further. If your money is used as a tool to steal from others, then it is your God-given right to not participate in the theft of others. In this way, Bitcoin is a civil rights movement.

On October 31, 1517, Martin Luther sparked what became the Reformation. On this day, he published the 95 theses which attacked the corrupt practices of the papacy and initiated a Protestant movement which separated Church from State and recognized voluntary, peer-to-peer relationship with God as a human right. On January 3, 1521, Luther was excommunicated from the Catholic Church for his protest.[61]

Satoshi Nakamoto sparked a Reformation movement on October 31, 2008. On this day, he published the nine-page Bitcoin whitepaper which attacked the corrupt practices of money manipulation and sparked a financial protestant movement that separated money from State and recognized voluntary peer-to-peer transactions as a human right. On January 3, 2009, Satoshi mined the first Bitcoin block.[62]

Whether the Keynesian Kings like it or not, the separation of money and State is happening in plain sight.

Math is relentless. When debt catches up to the dollar, the only way to save fiat money will be to peg it to bitcoin. Inevitable, whichever government agency is put in charge of maintaining the bitcoin peg will eventually break that trust.

When the working class awakes to find that their political currency units no longer buy anything of value, violence could sweep the streets. The most peaceful option for civilization's transition from abundant money to scarce money is to gradually adopt bitcoin through education and moral conviction.

From the country of El Salvador to the corporation of MicroStrategy, visionary pioneers are preparing for a better future with better money. A future where people refuse to work for money that others can create for free. A future where money is fair, transparent, and predictable. A future where central banks cannot hide and manipulate the rules of money to enrich insiders.

On a pure bitcoin standard, the game of interest rate manipulation will come to an end. No longer will the Keynesian Kings get to decide the price of money. No longer will political insiders get to decide who gets first access to newly printed money. The Cantillon effect game of using debt-printing privileges to buy scarce assets before inflation hits will come to an end.

A free market economy needs free market money. When the Federal Reserve gets to decide when to lower interest rates, they cause asset prices to go up. When the Federal Reserve decides to raise interest rates, they cause asset prices to go down. These repricing cycles create lucrative buying and selling opportunities that enrich insiders, but this type of money supply manipulation has horrific costs on the productivity, health, and well-being of the working class.

John Maynard Keynes was wrong. Printing money does not create wealth; it only redistributes wealth to people who are closer to the money printer. What happens to an economy when people refuse to work for money that Keynesian Kings can print for free? In this next chapter, we will count the costs of an unpredictable money supply, so we can imagine the benefits of building an economy on a predictable money supply.

2

ECONOMICS

"And the cost of a thing, it will be remembered, is the amount of life it requires to be exchanged for it, immediately or in the long run."[63] —Henry David Thoreau, *The Writings of Henry David Thoreau.*

Your life on Earth is limited. As the cost of living goes up, you must exchange more of your life to keep up.

Better technology saves time and reduces costs. Have you ever asked yourself, why are prices still going up?

The truth is prices aren't going up; the value of your dollars are going down. The denominator of your money is being printed to infinity.

From 1898 to 1974, Campbell's Condensed Tomato Soup averaged about $0.10 per can.[64] After more than 70 years of stable prices, President Nixon suspended the gold exchange rate for the US dollar. Fast-forward 50 years and without gold anchoring down prices, the price of tomato soup has risen to over $1.00 per can. A 10x price increase would not be so alarming if personal income grew by a similar rate, but did it?

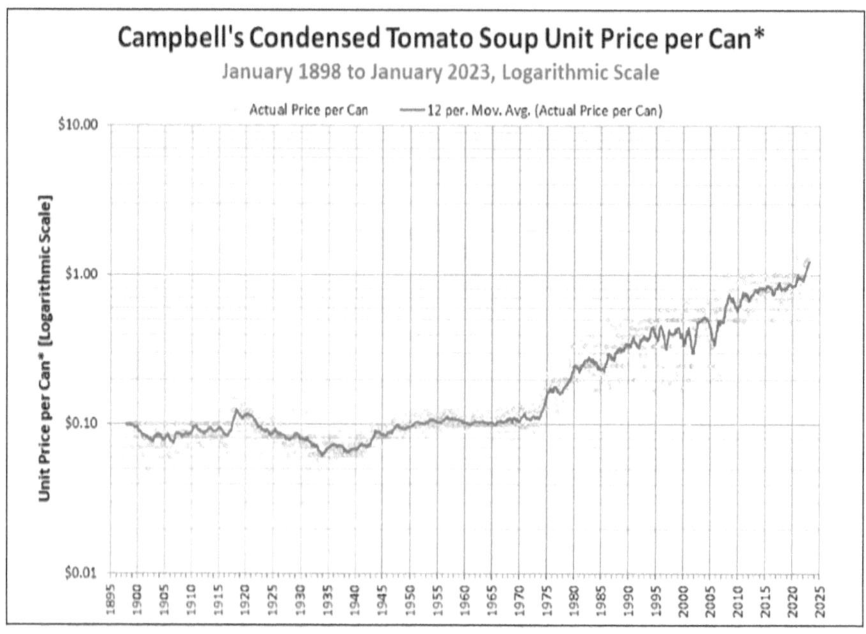

Source: Political Calculations 2023[64]

From 1974 to 2021, US median income (after taxes) grew from \$4,276 to \$28,869:

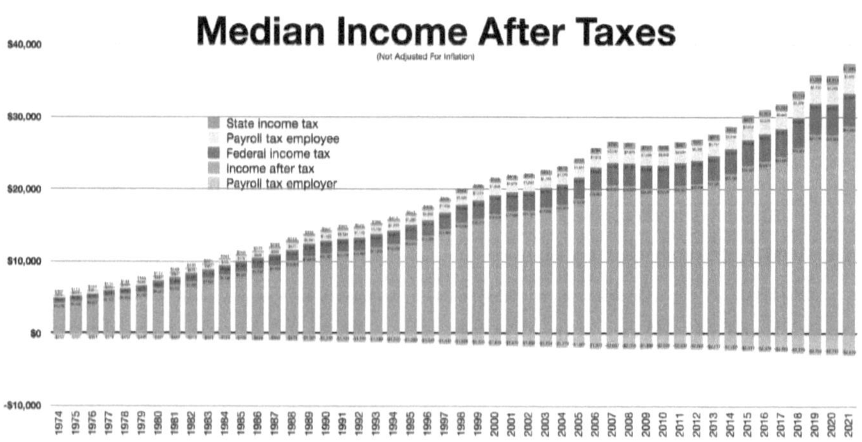

Source: WikiMedia.[65]

On the surface, a 6.75 times increase in take-home income sounds fantastic! However, when you consider your cans of tomato soup have gone up in price by over 10 times, it doesn't seem that good anymore. When you consider that the total money supply is 30 times larger, it's starting to look a lot like a pay cut. The working class' share of the fiat money pie has shrunk. Let's crack open a can of tomato soup to warm things up.

From 1974 to 2021, software, robotics, and industrial farming have made it much easier to manufacture a can of tomato soup. How much more tomato soup can you buy today thanks to this better technology? The truth is that with his or her income in 2021 a worker can afford to buy 13,891 fewer cans of tomato soup per year than a worker could in 1974. The Keynesian Kings have stolen 32% tomato soup purchasing power from the working class. However, the truth is that better technology has reduced the human work required to make a can of tomato soup, so with hard money like bitcoin the price of tomato soup would have been much less than $0.10.

The price of tomato soup is simple evidence that the Keynesian Kings are printing fiat money to steal your purchasing power.

Here is the key point of this chapter. Technology is deflationary. Better technology reduces manual labor and optimizes supply chains which puts downward pressure on costs over time. The cost of living should be going down, not up. Why, then, is your cost of living going up?

Since President Nixon abandoned the Bretton Woods' gold standard in 1971, the US dollar supply (as measured by M2) has grown by 6.9% per year, from $710.3 billion up to $21.5 trillion.[66] Over the last 50 years, every company that failed to reduce their costs by 6.9% per year had to raise prices. Campbell failed to reduce its annual tomato soup costs by 6.9%, so their prices went up. If your annual raise was less than 6.9%, then less soup for you.

1971 COST OF LIVING

LIVING

New House	$25,200.00
Average Income	$10,622.00 per year
New Car	$3,560.00
Average Rent	$150.00 per month
Tuition to Harvard University	$2,600.00 per year
Movie Ticket	$1.50 each
Gasoline	40¢ per gallon
United States Postage Stamp	8¢ each

FOOD

Granulated Sugar	62¢ for 5 pounds
Vitamin D Milk	$1.17 per gallon
Ground Coffee	98¢ per pound
Bacon	80¢ per pound
Eggs	45¢ per dozen
Fresh Ground Hamburger	62¢ per pound
Fresh Baked Bread	25¢ per loaf

Source: Little House.[67]

What can you do to protect yourself from 6.9% dollar destruction per year?

A financial advisor will advise you to buy assets, but which assets?

Let's look at 50-year asset returns adjusted for President Nixon's dollar destruction.

Post-Gold Standard, Annual Asset Returns:

(US) M2 Money Supply:[68]
1971: $710.3 billion
2021: $21,549.2 billion
Money Supply Expansion = 30.3x
Annual Dollar Destruction = 6.9%

#1) S&P 500 Index:[69]
1971: 103.29
2021: 4,766.18
Annual Return = 7.8%
Adjusted for Dollar Destruction = 0.9% per year

#2) Dow Jones Industrial Average:[70]
1971: 890.2
2021: 36,338.3
Annual Return = 7.7%
Adjusted for Dollar Destruction = 0.8% per year

#3) US 10 Year Treasury Bond:[71]
1970s: 5.4%
1980s: 11.9%
1990s: 7.7%
2000s: 6.9%
2010s: 5.5%
Annual Compound Rate = 7.5%
Adjusted for Dollar Destruction = 0.6% per year

#4). US Median Home Price:[72]
1971: $25,500
2021: $423,600
Annual Return = 5.7%
Adjusted for Dollar Destruction = -1.2% per year

#5) Gold[73]
1971: $37.44
2021: $1,940.35
Annual Return = 8.0%
Adjusted for Dollar Destruction = 1.1% per year

During the last 50 years of dollar destruction, real estate was the worst way to save your money from debasement. If you bought gold before 1980 or gambled your wages in the stock market, you may have timed markets to come out slightly ahead of dollar debasement. For those lucky enough to escape dollar destruction, a final capital gains tax was levied to negate your escape. The Keynesian Kings are at war with savings.

Successfully trading stocks, bonds, real estate, and gold to escape dollar destruction boils down to correctly timing your buy and sell orders based on market conditions. Wall Street pays top dollar for inside information about money printing, board meetings, pending regulations, and political legislation. The working class is not privileged to the same information as this well-staffed group of Keynesian Kings. If you do get lucky with your investments, you are still taxed on capital gains. For this reason, the multibillion dollar inflation industry was born to help you "save" your money from inflation **only if** you wait to cash out until retirement.

An army of financial advisors has been enlisted by the Keynesian Kings to help you save for retirement during the destruction of your dollars. The inflation industry is not about investing to grow your purchasing power over time; it is about paying a team of insiders to beat inflation for you. In fact, the average 401(k) returns between 5-8% per year at a cost of 0.25%-0.5% fees.[74] And if you time your retirement just right, over 30 years, you might pay $20,000 in 401(k) fees *just* to keep your purchasing power intact.

It is responsible to save for retirement. The problem is saving for retirement with broken money forces you to invest in Wall Street.

Your auto-pilot 401(k) contributions keep zombie companies on life support while injecting economic inflation with steroids. As a blind working-class investor in the stock market, money managers use a reliable portion of your paycheck to fund mega-corporations. Your paycheck gets spent on corporate lobbying, political CEOs, and other types of civil corruption that you would never buy if it weren't for inflation and retirement tax incentives.

Your financial advisor may brag that your stock portfolio went up with stock buybacks, but most fail to mention that half of all stock buybacks are the result of new debt creation.[75] That's right, trillions of new dollars are created by corporations to buy back their own stock to benefit their stock price. The debt-fueled stock buyback problem clouds the market's ability to judge a company by its merits and also increases inflation.

If the retirement industry's sole purpose of beating inflation sounds wasteful to you, then I'd like to welcome you to a new way of thinking.

THE FUTURE IS NOT FIAT MONEY

It is time to rethink the future economy in which you hope to retire.

The future economy will be digital with advancements in digital technologies that naturally reduce the overall demand for human labor. For example, from 1991 to 2021, the *market cap per employee* at Apple has risen by 37 times, jumping from $406,049 to $15.09 million per employee. The digital trend shows fewer employees are needed to run technology-focused companies like Apple.[76]

As car manufacturers self-insure their self-driving vehicles, how many car insurance agents will be out of work? As virtual meeting rooms replace commercial office buildings, how many local restaurants, cleaning services, and dry cleaners will go out of business? If the future economy is made up of more technology-focused companies like Apple, will decreasing human labor demand be a good thing or a bad thing for society?

It depends. Technologies like machine learning, automation, robotics, and Bitcoin make it harder for humans to add value in the workplace.

The nightmare scenario is continued inflation as we shift further into a deflationary digital economy. If the Keynesian Kings prevent prices from falling for the working class, then more people will give up on honest work and seek help from the State. As the State grows more powerful from the strings of welfare programs, politicians will need to extract more productivity gains from the economy through inflation and taxation.

This negative feedback loop caused by broken money is like a dark form of gravity pulling the world into a dystopian future.

Thankfully, a better option exists. If the working class wants a free market economy that runs on free market money, then bitcoin is the better option. If money creation is separated from the State, then humanity is more likely to avoid a dystopian future. As more people switch from fiat-based investments to saving their work in bitcoin, better technology will reduce all prices in bitcoin terms. In turn, a drop in prices reduces the amount of work required for you to fund your desired lifestyle.

As Bitcoin skeptics see their friends, family, and neighbors benefit, I am optimistic that incentives will wake people up to the idea of using better money for the hope of building a better world. Economies belong to the people who work in them, not the politicians who micromanage them. The working class holds the real proof-of-work power that runs the fiat economy. When workers choose honest money for honest trade, lasting change will happen.

Money printers are battling economic physics. Time is not on the side of the Keynesian Kings. In less than a decade, the US dollar has dropped over 99.8% in value against bitcoin. The scarcity of bitcoin is illuminating the fragility of our debt-based system. More people are seeing the flaws of fiat money and noticing the opportunity to use bitcoin as a better savings account to grow their long-term purchasing power.

How can bitcoin be a savings account when its price is so unstable? An unstable free-market price with growing adoption is better than a stable, centrally planned price with declining adoption. Short-term price instability is the price bitcoin savers pay for the long-term rewards of being early. Fully adopted, the unstable dollar price of bitcoin will disappear and be replaced by a stable repricing of everything in bitcoin.

When will this happen? The dollar was used in 75% of all 2022 global trade.[77] In the future, do you think more people around the world will use dollars or bitcoin to transact within an increasingly digital economy? The answer to this question can help you decide how to save your money.

Is the end of the dollar near? Maybe. America overprinted in response to the COVID-19 pandemic, blocked Russia from using dollars on the SWIFT network, and froze 300 billion in dollar reserves from Russian banks.[78] American politicians, drunk on printing power, accelerated global abandonment of the dollar as the world's reserve currency. Foreign nations can no longer rely on American permission to protect their wealth.

Proverbs 16:18 says, pride comes before destruction, a haughty spirit before a fall. American pride, political censorship, and intentional inflation has broken the dollar as a reliable measuring stick of value. In the next chapter, we dive deep into the political ramifications and paradigm shift away from political money and towards neutral money. Now let's unpack the idea of money being used as a measuring stick of value.

ENGINEERED ECONOMIC CHAOS

"But money should always be money. A foot is always twelve inches, but when is a dollar a dollar? If ton weights changed in the coal yard, and peck measures changed in the grocery, and yard sticks were to-day 42 inches and to-morrow 33 inches (by some occult process called "exchange") the people would mighty soon remedy that. When a dollar is not always a dollar, when the 100-cent dollar becomes the 65-cent dollar, and then the 50-cent dollar, and then the 47-cent dollar, as the good old American gold and silver dollars did, what is the use of yelling about "cheap money,"

"depreciated money"? A dollar that stays 100 cents is as necessary as a pound that stays 16 ounces and a yard that stays 36 inches."
—Henry Ford, *My Life and Work.*[79]

My brother is a structural engineer. I asked him one evening, "If a group of politically appointed engineers changed the measurement of a meter to be longer or shorter every month, how would that impact your work?" He confessed that the costs of reworking his calculations would be wasteful and annoying. If a meter was 1.2 meters next month and 1.3 meters next year, then inconsistent calculations and communication errors between architects, engineers, and construction crews would cause many buildings to crumble.

Being a proponent of an elastic money supply is like supporting an elastic meter. Unpredictable money supply has a price — economic chaos.

Repricing an entire economy based on the manipulated cost of fiat money creation has destroyed the working class. First, low interest rates to print new money lures working people into the dream of owning assets for passive income. When asset markets get too hot, retail investors are crushed by deflation shocks as the Federal Reserve is forced to restore confidence in the purchasing power of the cheaply printed and now more abundant dollars. The human costs of boom-bust-bailout cycles are suicides, broken families, and a stressed-out workforce. Faith, family, and fitness all take a backseat to finance; this deteriorates the culture.

The boom-bust-bailout cycle is not a natural phenomenon in economics; it is a side effect of manipulated money. On the gold standard, boom-bust-bailout cycles happened as gold owners could not easily take self-custody of their gold coins and banks overprinted IOU gold notes. On the fiat standard, boom-bust-bailout cycles happen as paper owners cannot easily take self-custody of their paper cash and banks overprint digital IOUs. With widespread self-custody possible on a bitcoin standard, the boom-bust-bailout cycles may become a thing of the past.

How can we peacefully transition our economy to a more stable bitcoin standard? The cornerstone of sustainable bitcoin adoption must be moral conviction. People who do real work in the economy must vote for bitcoin with their wages. When the working class refuses to work for fiat money that the Keynesian Kings can create without work, the reward for society will be better economics.

One day, the idea of buying scarce bitcoin with abundant fiat money will be viewed as the ultimate act of arbitrage. As if by design, during this generational shift in money technology, bitcoin volatility has the overlooked benefit of destroying short-term greed and rewarding long-term savings. The savers who understand bitcoin will hold it through the price swings and end up reaping the full benefits of bitcoin as a savings tool.

Bitcoin represents a shift from physical money to digital money. On a smaller scale, Amazon represented a shift from physical shopping to digital shopping. If you bought Amazon stock in November 1999, you paid $4.25 per share. Before enjoying $164.25 per Amazon share in September 2021, you had to first survive your Amazon shares dropping to $0.30 in September 2001.[80] Early Amazon investors who believed in the company's vision used the price dips as opportunities to acquire more shares in Amazon, not to sell based on US dollar price swings.

Bitcoin is an early-stage money technology that represents just 0.43% of the value of all global fiat currencies in 2023.[81] Bitcoin is an undervalued idea. Most don't consider that the addressable market of bitcoin reaches far beyond replacing global fiat currencies. As a digital store of value, bitcoin can take market share from a range of physical assets that are purchased by investors as monetary tools to beat inflation.

Most real estate investments, artwork, Treasury bonds, and stocks fall short of directly improving the standard of living for most investors. Wealthy people buy these types of scarce assets to simply protect themselves from inflation and increase their purchasing power over time. With bitcoin as a better savings tool, high-net-worth investors' demand for non-essential assets to beat inflation will drop.

As bitcoin absorbs the monetary premiums for non-money assets, the cost to buy real estate, artwork, bonds, and stocks will decline over time. This makes bitcoin an engineered digital savings account that increases your ability to purchase scarce non-money assets. As bitcoin adoption grows around the globe, exchange rates will stabilize, and growth in bitcoin purchasing power will align to growth in global productivity gains.

How far along is bitcoin in its adoption cycle? In 2023, 11.7 million addresses held 0.01 or more bitcoin.[82] This means less than 0.14% of the world's 8.1 billion population held more than 1 million satoshis, or about $300 worth of bitcoin in July of 2023. The real percentage is much lower; like email, most people have multiple Bitcoin addresses, and 0.14% Bitcoin adoption double counts the unique people with multiple addresses of more than 1 million satoshis.

In 2014, 2018, and 2022, bitcoin had annual price drops of 82%, 83%, and 77% against the US dollar.[83] The Bitcoin network continued to operate as normal during these price drops, so it is better to view these price swings as changes in *adoption*, not in the quality of the Bitcoin network.

Over the first 12 years of open exchange, the US dollar has only beaten bitcoin in 3 out of 12 years. In fact, the US dollar has lost 99.88% of its purchasing power versus bitcoin over the last ten years. Bitcoin is not a bubble: When bubbles pop they don't come back. Bitcoin has come back stronger after every price drop. Bitcoin is not a fad; it is the future of money following a four-year adoption cycle.

Do you still fear you are too late to learn Bitcoin? Everyone feels late to Bitcoin. One more fact to overcome that fear is that in 2022 there were 62.5 million US-dollar millionaires globally.[84] If every one of those 62.5 million millionaires wanted to own a whole bitcoin, that would be mathematically impossible. The most each millionaire could theoretically own is 0.336 bitcoin per millionaire. However, when you consider that 20% of the total bitcoin supply was lost in the early days and 50% will most likely be held by governments and public companies, then it is more like 0.1335 bitcoin per millionaire.

After seeing the math, do you still believe Bitcoin has reached its full potential? Regardless, remember an important point from the last chapter. Just like the wheel, fire, electricity, and the internet, you are not too late to adopt better technology. You can use bitcoin as a better savings account today and be better off for that decision by tomorrow.

I used to think bitcoin adoption was an IQ test, but now I feel it is more of a humility test. It takes a humble person to admit they have worked for bad money their entire life. Everyone gets bitcoin at the price when they admit they were wrong about bitcoin.

Our digital economy is moving to digital money whether we like it or not. Everyone will choose between a State-controlled digital currency or bitcoin. The earlier you make your choice, the more time you will have to build your future on that choice.

THE RENAISSANCE OF SAVING

Renaissance means rebirth. Historically, the Renaissance described the transition from Medieval times to modern times. What if we are living through an economic renaissance today? It is difficult to imagine a more dramatic shift in economic incentives than transitioning from an analog, debt-based economy to a digital, savings-based economy.

The fiat system incentivizes consumerism. As money supply growth pushes prices upwards, the "flash sale"-mentality to buy stuff quickly before prices go up has resulted in cultural habits of consumerism. If intentional inflation has created a "consumerism mindset" where abundant money chases scarce goods, then bitcoin can create a "savings mindset" where abundant goods chase scarce money. Money that rewards long-term thinking over instant gratification has the potential to naturally transition our culture away from consumerism.

What impact will this shift (from people chasing scarce goods to people chasing scarce money) have on our economy? Well, the prospect of earning money with greater future purchasing power can inspire abundant work and value creation across every sector of our economy. Instead of zombie companies surviving on debt privileges, only strong companies that provide more value than their competitors will stay in business. Transitioning from a debt-driven to a savings-driven economy will change the way we think about time, work, and spending money.

Let's talk about wages within a Bitcoin system. If money grows in value over time, will workers get a pay cut every year? To answer this common question, we must first understand an economic phenomenon called "sticky prices" and then we can talk about the concept of "sticky wages."

The best example of "sticky prices" can be found in your local grocery store. Food businesses don't know how much you will pay for a food product before you become disgruntled about the price and switch to a cheaper option. For food businesses planning supply chains and politicians planning re-election campaigns, your disgruntled switch of food products based on affordability is terrifying. To avoid food prices rising at the same rate as new money supply, food businesses may shrink your package sizes and politicians may allow the quality of your food ingredients to be reduced. While not good for your health, it is a subtle way to keep prices somewhat stable during money supply expansion.

On a bitcoin standard, the "sticky price" phenomenon would still exist, only in reverse. To avoid lowering prices, food businesses would grow package sizes and increase the quality of food ingredients. We explore the long-term impacts of how this change in food business incentives can improve your health in chapter 5. For this section, you only need to grasp the economic concept of a sticky price. Within a fiat system, producers cut costs to stabilize prices. Within a Bitcoin system, producers add value to stabilize prices.

If businesses and politicians despise the uncertainty created by adjusting prices, now consider the uncertainty created by cutting wages. Workers will be armed with a borderless bitcoin savings account and declining cost of living. If companies institute annual pay cuts, this will increase the likelihood and ability of workers to find better work elsewhere. Bitcoin incentives will drive a "sticky wage" phenomenon.

Within a sticky wage economy, a worker is hired at a salary in bitcoin and each passing year he or she remains valuable to the company, the worker is extended a pay increase by remaining hired at the same bitcoin salary. Rather than pay cuts each year, companies will attempt to add more value to their products per employee and cut employees who do not add value. This is like human resource management today, except workers would not be misled into believing a 5% pay raise is an increase when the fiat money supply is growing by 6.9% per year.

The psychological manipulation of workers' wages stolen by inflation is a sinister form of theft. The disguise of below-inflation annual pay raises in fiat money is dishonest economics at its worst. If the working class had really known how much their pay was being cut each year by intentional inflation, then governments and corporations would never have been allowed to behave so irresponsibly.

MEASURING INFLATION

To quell fiat money skepticism from "thinker brains" in society who want to discount inflation from their economic decisions, the Bureau of Labor Statistics, BLS, publishes a metric called the Consumer Price Index (CPI) as the official measurement of retail consumer inflation. Besides the obvious conflict in trusting a government department funded by the money printer to give you an accurate statistic on the damage it inflicts, the other major problem with this headline CPI number is that it falls short of capturing changes in human behavior due to price increases.

If families ate steak last year, but switched to ground beef this year due to affordability, guess what happens to the CPI metric? The steak is kicked out of the CPI basket of goods and replaced with the cheaper ground beef. To put downward pressure on the hyper-political headline CPI number, businesses either innovate to lower costs, lower quality, or take the risk of raising prices. Fiat money typically pushes quality off a cliff.

If not headline CPI, then what is the best way to measure inflation? Inflation is a vector; it cannot be measured accurately as an aggregate number like the CPI. Every person will have a different rate of inflation depending on what goods and services they want to buy.

Expansion of the money supply is weathered differently by different products, so it is best to measure inflation within specific products.

Unlike physical products, incumbent makers of digital products can add a million customers without paying much in additional costs. For example, a digital company like Netflix can profitably absorb monetary inflation without raising prices much due to their low marginal costs per customer. For technology companies, an often overlooked benefit of fiat money is how their marketing costs benefit from inflation. Within a fiat money system, the marketing costs a competitor must pay to take market share away from a big tech company increases over time. In this subtle scheme, fiat money finances the walls of network effects to grow higher for big tech companies over time. This is why, despite all of the breaches of privacy and trust, there will likely not be a better Facebook, Amazon, Apple, Netflix, or Google on a fiat money standard.

On the other hand, local farmers, due to high marginal costs, cannot profitably absorb monetary inflation without raising prices. Customers of farmers cannot be shielded from the price hikes of animal feed, veterinary care, fertilizer, and labor. Inflation rears its ugly head in different ways based upon differences in marginal costs for different business models. This is why prices for technology go down and prices for tomato soup go up.

Inflation is a personal metric that varies based on individual demand. A single man who inherits a house and wants to spend his paycheck on Netflix and Spicy Cheese Puffs will have a different inflation rate than a married man who wants to buy a single-family home and spend his paycheck on nutritional food. The closest thing we have to a uniformly in-demand, scarce product to measure inflation is real estate.

If Spicy Cheese Puffs are not your thing, affordable housing is likely a spicy topic you *do* care about. It is interesting to look at the rise in residential real estate prices through the lens of money supply inflation. In 1971, the median American household income was $10,285 and the median sales price of a house was $25,500.[85] This meant it took an American family 2.5 years' worth of wages to save up for a home.

Fast forward and you can see 50-years' worth of working class pay cuts in plain sight. In 2021, the median American household income was $88,590 and the median sales price of a house was $423,600. Now it takes an American family 4.8 years' worth of wages to buy a house.

Has better building technology lowered the marginal costs of home construction? Yes. How much more income have working moms added to household incomes? A lot. Nothing shows the theft of inflation more clearly than a 92% increase in the time it takes to save for a home.

Within the fiat money system, housing is the closest thing we have to uniform demand of a limited-supply asset. While engineers can expand the supply of housing by building residential skyscrapers, it is very expensive to expand the supply of habitable land for building the foundations of those skyscrapers. Apart from luxurious real estate projects, the cost required to "print land" by creating man-made islands is not economically feasible for the working class. Therefore, as more dollars are printed, working-class real estate prices in dollars have to go up.

Bitcoin is better real estate. Unequal access to debt, immobility, property taxes, maintenance costs, political protection requirements, an unknown supply and a narrow buyers' market all make real estate a complex and unreliable common denominator for economic value.

Bitcoin is the discovery of unprintable digital real estate for your money. Nothing like Bitcoin has ever existed before. Critics often repeat the line of attack that bitcoin has no intrinsic value, but they fail to understand the importance of scarcity and the simple expectations people have for the performance of their money. We don't need our money to cure cancer, sparkle in the light, or to become edible or habitable during difficult times. We need our money to serve as an economic battery for our work, so we can buy and sell things when we need them in the future.

On planet Earth, oxygen has more intrinsic value to human life than gold, so why is oxygen free to breathe and gold is not free to own? In environments where oxygen is scarce — like underwater or in outer space — people will pay for oxygen tanks. If abundant gold reserves are found on Earth or in outer space, the price people pay for gold will go down. Scarcity is what drives value in a healthy economy, not intrinsic value.

If bitcoin has a capped supply of less than 21 million, then why not create a cryptocurrency with a supply cap of 10 million coins to be more scarce and therefore more valuable? This common critique is overlooking network effects. Bitcoin is already a secure and globally accepted cryptographic language for value. Attempting to re-create a new Bitcoin to compete with the proven and highly secure Bitcoin won't work.

The network effects of Bitcoin make it theoretically impossible for any cryptocurrency to catch up and compete with the Bitcoin protocol. Millions of people have agreed upon the rules of Bitcoin, so to ask active bitcoin savers to abandon the existing rules that hold their money and start over in a new protocol would be foolish. Economic incentives do not exist for a better bitcoin.

Bitcoin is better money since it is verifiably scarcer than fiat money. It is a digital savings account that can be taken into self-custody without violence and moved across borders without political permission. Our ability to foresee the effects of a borderless savings-based economy built on top of scarce digital money are limited. Instead, we must ask better questions and use our imaginations to foresee this future together.

A FUTURE CONVERSATION

To better see the truth it is sometimes better to step back from reality. Fiction can be helpful to look beyond our biased worldview and think about the changes happening right in front of us. To personalize a future economy on a bitcoin standard, I am going to share a fictional conversation with Alex from the year 2100. I want you to imagine interviewing someone from the year 2100 and ask questions of your friend about living and working in a Bitcoin economy. This will help you identify the pros and cons of taking money creation out of human hands.

What is it like to work in a bitcoin-based economy?

ALEX: The purchasing power of bitcoin is pegged to global productivity gains. This means the brightest minds in society are no longer wasting their talents on building complex financial products to beat inflation. Medicine, energy, and engineering are far more attractive and financially rewarding fields than finance. When productivity breakthroughs happen, everyone celebrates because their bitcoin buys more things and becomes more valuable. The Bitcoin economy is like a collaborative competition to lower costs and raise the living standards for everyone.

What is it like to buy things in a bitcoin-based economy?

ALEX: Instead of inflationists stealing productivity gains, productivity gains from better technology are returned to the people through the appreciation of their bitcoin savings account. Every year the prices for most housing, transportation, food, and energy go down by 2-4%. To keep prices stable, all businesses compete to add more value to their products. In 2100, credit cards are obsolete technology. Transactions over the Lightning payment network mean businesses are no longer paying 3% fees to use credit cards. People freely send value across the globe at the speed of light without asking permission from banks or governments. The free market has been unchained to deliver higher-quality products at lower costs. This financial freedom is better for everyone.

If Bitcoin settlements are final, what is it like to try to get a refund without a bank or credit card company?

ALEX: Since the money is no longer a lie, we have a more honest economy. It is rare for a customer to try to rip off a business or a business to try to rip off a customer. Online reviews are verified to be human by bitcoin deposits and carry much more weight than they used to under the fiat system. If a business doesn't treat its customers with respect, it does not continue to operate. Bitcoin raised the cost of malice in the economy.

What is it like to issue debt within a Bitcoin system?

ALEX: A free market for borrowing and lending is used by governments and businesses for large projects. The interest rates for all loans are set in real time by the supply of lenders and the demand from borrowers. There are professional services that vet risks for loans. Their business model is based on keeping a transparent track record of reliable loan performance. For small loans, peer-to-peer lending through time-locked contracts is the preferred method. Both parties sign terms and automatically set rates on the Lightning payment network.

How does a Bitcoin economy grow without growing the money supply?

ALEX: The big lie of the "too big to fail" fractional reserve banks was that the quantity of money must grow for the economy to grow. Before being stripped of their privileges to fractionally reserve bitcoin notes, the bankers argued that new businesses could not operate without their ability to create new money to fund loans. These banks became obsolete after this argument fell apart. On a fiat system, the truth was that fully reserved lending — like venture capital and private equity — funded new businesses, and fractional reserve banking kept zombie companies alive. People realized that bitcoin could be divided into infinitely small decimal values to provide enough liquidity for a growing economy.

How has Bitcoin mining impacted energy prices?

ALEX: For over 100 years, an infinite supply of fiat money funded an infinite stream of misallocated resources which polluted the planet. Bitcoin returned the world to a real cost of capital through its proof-of-work protocol. This unlocked Moore's law for clean energy production. We now see a doubling in energy storage capacity every 18 months. The proof-of-work protocol behind Bitcoin allowed inventors to fund development of battery technology by monetizing stranded energy. Engineers found new ways to convert abundant natural energy resources into abundant electricity for everyone. With expanded access to cheap energy, the living standards for everyone on the planet improve each and every year. Bitcoin mining helped connect the power grid to stranded energy from the sun, wind, ocean tides, and volcanoes.

What is it like working alongside AI on a bitcoin standard?

ALEX: Instead of calling it artificial intelligence, we call it a learning machine agent (LMA). Artificial intelligence requires emotional intelligence, which is an impossible programming task within an LMA algorithm. Emotional intelligence is unique to human beings. That being said, before bitcoin was globally adopted there was a serious challenge with deep fake videos. Presidential videos were deep faked by warmongers, CEO videos were deep faked by short-sellers, and celebrity videos were deep faked by scammy advertisers. On the bitcoin standard, all media devices automatically authenticate content by verifying the Bitcoin private key (BPK) of the original publisher. The more BPK confirmations by those portrayed in the video, the more confidence viewers have that the media is authentic. Bitcoin cryptography helps us keep the machines honest.

How is privacy protected when using the public ledger of Bitcoin?

ALEX: The greatest hurdle to libertarian-leaning circles adopting bitcoin was the public nature of the Bitcoin ledger. There was a well-founded concern that oppressive governments may require citizens to register their Bitcoin public addresses so authoritarians could track transactions and control commerce. At one point in time, there was a debate over whether or not to build a programmable central bank digital currency on top of Bitcoin to better "protect" privacy. Thankfully, my grandparents' generation saw the red flags, rejected it, and created better solutions. Today all bitcoin storage devices mix coins before publishing a public transaction. For offline transactions, physical bitcoin packets with verifiably unused private keys are traded like anonymous paper cash transactions. Bitcoin is a public protocol that supports privacy layers built on top of it.

What is it like to buy a house within a Bitcoin system?

ALEX: The old French term for "death pledge" that you call a mortgage is obsolete. Instead of pledging debt until death, people use their bitcoin savings account to save up for their homes. The price of rents and homes drop about 2-4% per year, so people are motivated to reject wasteful spending to save up for their dream home. Since houses depreciate against bitcoin, real estate is treated as a utility and no longer seen as an investment. Real estate is treated like vehicles were treated under the fiat system: Most people do not expect to sell their home for more bitcoin after they use it. To ask the same bitcoin price year-after-year, buyers expect home builders to add more technology to their homes.

What advice would you give to people as they transition from fiat money to bitcoin?

ALEX: Don't get angry; get bitcoin. The money printers hold more power than you realize. Any excuse to crack down on the Bitcoin network will be exploited, so I recommend you take a peaceful approach in your resistance. The working class wants a solution, not another enemy. Allow the politicians room to squabble and stay focused on the big picture. Theft is wrong. Most people agree and just don't know it yet.

—

Welcome back to today. I hope this conversational exercise was helpful for you to imagine what an economy could look like on a bitcoin standard. There may come a day when the temptation of a central bank digital currency is presented to you. Resist the carrot. Whether it is universal basic income, stimulus, or even being granted permission to work based on political allegiance, just say no. Bitcoin is better.

CONCLUSION

If you want to spend less of your life at work, then rising prices should concern you.

Please don't mistake my point here since honest work is good: Honest work is how we serve others with our time, talents, and energy to make the world a better place. As we get better at making things, the price of things should get less expensive for everyone. Under a fiat money system, despite better work productivity from the working class, the amount of work you have to do to afford to buy things gets higher every year.

What is the point in working on a hamster wheel? Life is so much more than work. If you knowingly exchange your work for an unlimited currency, you are choosing to have your limited time and your limited energy stolen away from family, friends, fitness, faith, and fun.

If better technology reduces demand for your labor, it should also reduce your cost of living.

The jobs of the industrial revolution disappeared and are not coming back. The internet dematerialized the paper required to deliver the news. The job of the newspaper boy is gone. Google dematerialized libraries. Amazon dematerialized physical supply chains. The incoming digital economy needs deflationary money to offset the deflationary nature of this digital revolution.[86]

The old models are broken. Gross domestic product, better known as GDP, is an outdated metric based upon economic spending that fails to measure the growth in purchasing power as a result of better technology.

GDP (Y) = consumption (C) + investment (I) + government expenditures (G) + (exports(X) – imports(M))

Under a fiat system, growth is defined by GDP or gross spending plus net exports. Under a growing fiat money supply base, consumption is viewed as growth. Gauging economic health by GDP growth fails to capture a new type of growth called productivity gains, which is a net negative to GDP. The complicated and easily manipulated GDP metric must be replaced with some type of bitcoin purchasing power metric.

Think about it. Where do all your extra photos you take today show up in GDP? Where does all the extra music you listen to today show up in GDP? Where does the free calculator app you use on your phone instead of a store-bought one show up in GDP? Productivity gains drive down the GDP metric, so the idea that we can pay off hundreds of trillions of dollars' worth of debt with perpetual GDP growth is irrational at best.

At worst, GDP is a nefarious metric. You cannot grow the volume of consumption forever on a finite planet. When you try, you have more and more people working harder and harder on a hamster wheel that only makes the fiat system worse. Everything modern technology companies have touched has been deflationary, yet prices continue to rise. The money must be lying to us about prices.

When the money lies to us, the entire economy becomes built on lies. Price signals become political signals and the inertia of inflation crushes an uninformed working class. I think the most sinister part of this entire inflation scheme is that most working people have no clue it is even happening. You may think you are given an annual pay raise, when the truth is you are given a dishonest pay cut due to intentional inflation.

What will wake up working people to bitcoin as better money? It often takes a crisis to sharpen and focus the mind. During the mandated COVID-19 pandemic lockdowns, I discovered Bitcoin. I am still discovering new things about Bitcoin to this day. We must learn from our mistakes and try our best to avoid repeating the mistakes of our ancestors. The best harbingers are found in the dusty pages of old history books.

For an idea of where our world is heading after the COVID-19 pandemic, we should be learning from the political mistakes following the last global pandemic. The Spanish flu of 1918 killed an estimated 50 million people worldwide.[87] This global pandemic preluded hyper-inflation in 1920s Germany. As prices skyrocketed, leaders from the National Socialist Party convinced a minority of the German population that they were victims of Jewish bankers. The Nazis rose to power and Adolph Hitler was elected to lead a war against all supposed German oppressors.

My point is this. It doesn't matter who is blamed for the post-pandemic inflation this time around. Whether it is Jewish bankers, Democrats, Republicans, or bitcoin savers, the truth is no one is innocent within this broken system. We have all used credit cards, taken out mortgages, and voted for politicians who promise security and entitlements, yet in the process saddled future generations with trillions of dollars in debt.

Money should not be political. An entire economy hinging on what the Federal Reserve decides to do about the price of new money is the height of economic dysfunction. A debt system cannot be liberated with tools controlled by that same debt system. Our debt-based economy can only be liberated with a tool that is from outside of the control of our broken political system. That tool is Bitcoin.

Bitcoin can serve as a reliable productivity benchmark to accurately measure the impact of politics and technological innovations on our civilization. We live in a deflationary world, and we need a deflationary money that matches that reality. Instead of increasing consumption forever, the future goal of economics will be to reduce the cost of living for everyone and thereby improve the standard of living for everyone.

Next, we explore how the unprintable nature of bitcoin empowers the working class to hold politicians mathematically accountable for results.

3
POLITICS

If you seek the truth in politics, the straightest course to the truth is to follow the money.

As G.K. Chesterton wrote in *The Everlasting Man*, "A dead thing can go with the stream, but only a living thing can go against it."[89]

Are you prepared to paddle upstream to find the truth? Within politics, the great temptation is to float downstream with other dead things on the river of outrage. However, history is littered with well-intentioned revolutionaries who ride this lazy river over waterfalls of destruction.

Outrage is non-productive self-destruction. If you want to remain a living thing, if you desire peace, if you desire reconciliation, then you must put in the work to paddle upstream. Only after you find the toxic source of outrage can you contribute to cleaning it up.

At the source of this river we call government, you will find a leak in the form of toxic money. Fiat money is political pollution because it has no tether to reality. It is a distortion that deforms culture and pollutes politics downstream. When people get outraged at dysfunctional government, instead of blaming the polluters, voters are convinced to blame one another.

Whether intentional or by habit, the Keynesian Kings exploit a toxic leak of economic energy to steal work, enrich insiders, mask corruption, distort reality, and divide voters under the guise of partisanship.

Now that you have found the toxic leak of fiat money into politics, you can view political outrage through an entirely different lens. Whatever political problem you care most about, you will now begin to see how printing more dollars has made it worse.

How exactly has adding more units to the money supply caused more political outrage and division? Simple: The price of everything is wrong.

Price equilibrium balances supply and demand. When the Keynesian Kings print money, they purposefully break this natural equilibrium. The intentional destruction of working-class purchasing power gives those who control the money supply a supernatural ability to manipulate what is valued by our society. Money is not only a measurement for goods and services, but a measurement for our time and energy as well.

When the truth is absent from the money, truth will also be absent from most of society.

What is truth? For mortal men, mathematics is the globally accepted language of truth. If everyone worked for money that was based upon mathematics instead of political power, naturally this would be a force for peace in the world. Think about it. If money was spoken in the language of mathematics instead of politics, truth could set the world free to work together.

If fiat money is a lie about value, how does that lie influence politics?

Simply put, supply and demand have gone out the window. For example, you have an oversupply of politicians who campaign on distractions and name-calling rather than substance. Fiat money encourages politicians to divide, instead of diagnosing the root cause of real problems.

Centrally planned money supply has created centrally planned "capitalism" and left the entire global economy in a state of price confusion. If you try to divide goods and services by a denominator — called money — that is unpredictable and prone to corruption you get economic chaos.

The most subtle side effect of fiat money is distraction. Bad money is good at keeping you too busy and too distracted to notice that it is stealing from you. Price confusion has distracted voters from the costs of corrupt collaboration between government and corporations.

How does this collaboration work? Printed money prevents voters from feeling the short-term pain of bad politics. After printing new monetary units into existence, sticky prices typically hide money devaluation for 6 to 18 months. If increased labor and superior technology fails to increase the output of goods and services to match the increase of money supply, then prices rise faster than wages. Like killing a man slowly by feeding him candy for every meal, people are fed political outrage and slowly taxed to death through delayed inflation.

Inflation is a clever political trick that gives politicians the time and cover they need to blame others for the consequences of their bad ideas. Since fiat money funds government budgets there are no real-world costs to create new government capital, so there are no real-world costs for bad political ideas. If I had to put it on a t-shirt it would say: "Money divorced from reality has divorced politicians from reality."

Good leaders talk about real-world problems and offer practical solutions that leave you feeling optimistic. On the contrary, authoritarians want you to feel angry and hopeless about the future. Throughout history, authoritarians have pushed ideologies of fear and victimhood onto people they want to control. This makes sense when you understand that an optimistic population is nearly impossible to control.

If you lose hope in the possibility of honest work providing your family with a livable income, it creates an opportunity for money-printing authoritarians to exploit your despair for political gain. It is important to recognize divide-and-conquer tactics. These opportunists will try to entice you with promises of bigger welfare programs that will be paid for by your political enemies. It is a trap.

In reality, such promises lead only to further dependence on benevolent dictators. Here is the key takeaway of this section. Without the anchor of hope, working people will quickly descend from Patrick Henry's "Give me liberty or give me death" to a French Revolution chant of, "Tax the rich!" and "Off with their heads!" If you desire political freedom, placing your hope in a better future is not optional.

Jesus said, "Every kingdom divided against itself is brought to desolation, and every city or house divided against itself, shall not stand."[90] Class-warfare taxation is a tyrannical tactic and a popular divide-and-conquer strategy. Rich people are misled to believe that lazy poor people do not pay taxes. Poor people are misled to believe that lazy rich people do not pay taxes. This class-warfare strategy tears a nation apart.

According to the IRS in 2020, the top 50% of American earners paid 97.7% of total income taxes and nearly all of the capital gains taxes.[91] Before crying foul on unfair taxation, consider that the inflation tax impacts the price of basic needs (food, energy, and rent) more than luxurious items. This means poor people pay a disproportionately higher percentage of their income on the inflation tax than rich people.[92]

The truth is fiat money is robbing both the rich and the poor of their time, efforts, and resources. The rich sacrifice their mental sanity on complex investments to keep their fiat money, and the poor sacrifice their mental sanity on longer work hours to earn enough fiat money to survive. Bitcoin is better for everyone. It is a bipartisan, classless, unifying idea that can bring all people together.

THE TRUTH PANDEMIC

The COVID-19 crisis ripped the mask off of money printing to reveal the truth about taxes. Everyone who holds US dollars is a taxpayer.

From February 2020 to February 2022, the Federal Reserve printed over 6 trillion new US dollars in response to the COVID-19 pandemic.[93] By adding 40% more units into the total money supply within two years, the Keynesian Kings devalued all existing US dollar holders by 28% and sent workers small stimulus checks in return. Despite the quick and massive devaluation of the US dollar, 1.1 million Americans still died from or with COVID-19, childhood education was setback by one or two grade levels, and housing prices went up by 42%.[94]

Was it worth it? Let's look at the data. Haiti had a death rate of 8 deaths per 100,000, South Korea had a death rate of 67 deaths per 100,000, and the United States had a death rate of 341 deaths per 100,000.[95] Haiti was too poor to stimulate their economy, and South Korea did not lock down their economy. The data suggests devaluing US dollars by 28%, stunting children's education, mandating experimental vaccines to go to work, and locking people down in their homes did not save lives. It caused more suffering.

No one likes a Monday-morning quarterback, but it is unwise to let our inability to change the past become an excuse to avoid changing our future. Under the weight of fear and uncertainty, the COVID-19 pandemic exposed cracks in the foundation of our society built upon fiat money.

Fiscal responsibility was thrown out the window, and working-class families were forced to surrender 28% of their dollars' value through currency devaluation to pay for the government's war on COVID-19. Politicians cut working people $1.8 trillion in stimulus checks, and gave the other 2/3 of stimulus checks to businesses, corporations, and friends of the government.[96]

The biggest lesson I took away from the COVID-19 pandemic is all government spending requires taxation. Either taxes are knowingly taken from us through direct taxation or more national debt is created and the inflation tax is extracted from us without our consent.

In the eyes of uninformed voters, printing new political units of money from nothing creates the illusion of unlimited power. Politicians virtue signal by spending your money and pretending their infinite spending power gives them the right to control people who disagree with them. Political money is a tool of control, not trade. When you use money controlled by politicians, you give politicians permission to control you.

According to his biographer, American revolutionary James Otis said it best: Taxation without representation is tyranny.[97]

Did you vote for 30 times more US dollars over the last 50 years? Indirectly, yes; your representatives voted to raise the debt ceiling and allowed banks to print more money. Sadly, the complexity and deception of fiat politics prevents most people from connecting the dots on this scheme.

Most people would never break into their neighbor's house and steal cash from their safe, yet uninformed voters are conditioned to vote for politicians who promise to steal their neighbors' savings on their behalf. Whether through targeted taxation or dollar devaluation, taxation without consent from the taxpayer is theft.

Whether it is Wall Street lobbying politicians for higher inflation taxes on the poor to boost their asset prices, or the poor lobbying politicians for Wall Street to pay their fair share, the evidence is clear: Fiat politics is tearing us apart.

The rich, poor, and middle class are electing politicians who run for office on redistributing wealth from other classes to their voter base. A better money could help unite all economic classes of people to work together towards one goal: Adopting bitcoin to lower the cost of living for everyone.

Before we discuss why Bitcoin is better politics, we must first briefly discuss the system which replaced the failed gold standard.

THE BLACK GOLD STANDARD

I must admit to a concern, I have never had adequate answers about why we flew a plane load of Saudis out of this country right after 9/11, even though most of the hijackers were Saudis. When the FBI testified here, they said, well, we had FBI agents go in and talk to them before they took off. I asked if any FBI agents spoke Arabic. Of course, none did. We are far too cozy with the country that has provided the terrorists who have hit us here.[98] —Senator Patrick Leahy, US Senate Hearing before the Committee on the Judiciary.

Why does politics feel so disconnected from the real world?

The left wing believes the right wing is "conserving" corrupt corporations. The right wing believes the left wing is "progressing" toward global communism. What if we are looking at two wings of the same bird? What if left versus right is little more than political theater? John Adams warned against a two-party system: "a division of the republic into two great parties… is to be dreaded as the great political evil."[99]

The danger of two-party government is that it intensifies partisanship and lessens debate. Without diversity of thought, citizens are left with political theater that creates the illusion of voter choice. What if behind the scenes there is a unified party of corruption motivated by fiat money printing? If you follow the money trail of political campaigns, you will see why political division is good for corporate profitability.

Let's start with the corporate media. Campaign cash buys political ads on corporate media airwaves. The eyeballs of angry, uninformed voters are more easily swayed by political ads than a peaceful well-informed voter population. Rather than inform you, most corporate media is designed to startle you. Inflation removes the immediate pain of direct taxation for bad policy. The numbing effect of fiat money makes political gossip more profitable for corporate media than substantive debates about policy.

How does fiat money numb the pain of bad politics? America is the only country in the world that can print dollars to buy oil, price it in dollars, and thereby extract value from foreign countries. The privilege to print energy without work has created conflict around the globe and distorted our economy. Easy money has transformed Americans from hard-working creators into debt-laden consumers. This is the Black Gold Standard.

It's time to revisit the collapse of the 1944 Bretton Woods Gold Exchange Standard, so we can better understand its replacement.

During the 1960s, US President Lyndon B. Johnson enacted his vision for the Great Society. As we discovered in chapter 1, the goal of the LBJ agenda was to end poverty, reduce crime, abolish inequality, and improve the environment. These new and wildly underfunded socialist safety net programs like Medicare and Medicaid, in combination with the $200 billion Vietnam War, led to the collapse of the Bretton Woods system.

Foreign nations who once trusted gold reserves to back the US dollar knew extreme currency devaluation would be necessary to fund future American welfare and warfare deficit spending. In the wake of the monetary collapse, US President Richard Nixon and Secretary of State Henry Kissinger devised a plan to transition the global economy from a failed <u>dollars-for-gold</u> system to a more flexible <u>dollars-for-oil</u> system.

In 1974 Saudi Arabia agreed to denominate all oil reserves in US dollars and save surplus funds from oil sales in US Treasury bonds. In exchange for using the US dollar system, Americans would buy oil from the Saudis, sell weapons, and promise protection of Saudi oil fields from neighboring nations, including Israel.[100] To avoid mutually assured political destruction, details of this "Milestone Pact" were kept secret.

Saudi Arabia's King Faisal feared his citizens would view pricing oil in US dollars and buying US debt as indirectly supporting Israel. To provide the Saudis political cover, the American government agreed to modify country-by-country breakdowns of US debt ownership reporting. The Nixon administration agreed to group Saudi Arabia with 14 other nations under the generic heading of "oil exporters."[101]

US Secretary of State, Henry Kissinger, feared political backlash from European allies who failed to negotiate a similar agreement with Saudi Arabia to buy oil with their sovereign fiat currencies. In America, the pro-Israel voting bloc — mostly Republican evangelicals — would be outraged at a Republican administration's backroom deal to dictate Israeli foreign policy on behalf of Saudi Arabia. While the details of this handshake security contract between the United States and Saudi Arabia remained under lock and key, the results were quite obvious.

By 1975, all OPEC nations had followed Saudi Arabia's lead and agreed to dollarize their oil markets in exchange for weapons contracts and military protection. The Black Gold Standard replaced the Bretton Woods gold system and created an immediate boom of artificial demand for US dollars across the globe. As a result of politically binding US dollars to oil, 88% of all global currency trades now involve US dollars.[102]

Since the 1970s, global demand for US dollars has grown in lockstep with global demand for oil. Fifty years later, other nations are asking why.

Why is the US dollar being used in trillions of dollars of trades that have nothing to do with American products or services? BRICS nations (Brazil, Russia, India, China, and South Africa) are beginning to view the US dollar as a middleman currency. To foreign countries, the US dollar looks like an American scheme to export inflation abroad to pay for deficit spending at home. Let's look at the data.

1971: $3.50 or 0.08 gold ounces per barrel of oil.
2021: $75.00 or 0.04 gold ounces per barrel of oil.

Oil traded at $3.50 per barrel in 1971, and $75 per barrel in 2021. Over 50 years, oil got 21 times more expensive priced in dollars.

Oil traded at 0.08 gold ounces per barrel in 1971, and 0.04 gold ounces per barrel in 2021. Over 50 years, oil got 2 times cheaper priced in gold.

In 1971, $100 got you almost 29 barrels of oil, but in 2021 only one and a third. Fifty years after Nixon abandoned gold-backed money, why did the cost of a barrel of oil become 21 times more expensive in dollars compared with two times cheaper when priced in gold ounces?

If you compare the money supply from 1971 to 2021, there were 30 times more US dollars and only 2.7 times more gold ounces in circulation. The takeaway: Holders of scarcer money (gold) have been rewarded with productivity gains from better oil-extraction technology.

If you hold an abundant money (fiat), the people who print your money benefit as technology makes goods and services easier to bring to market. If you hold a scarce money, you benefit from cheaper prices as technology makes goods and services easier to bring to market.[103]

On a scarce money standard, technological tailwinds drive prices lower for everyone.

The overarching point of this math exercise is to show how the Black Gold Standard has inflamed global conflicts around the world. I believe the privilege to print money to buy energy is a bad deal for the United States and Saudi Arabia. Instead of working together to lower prices and increase the standard of living for everyone, fights over money printing privileges have transformed our world into a per-petual cycle of wars.

How did the dollars-for-oil system instigate the 9/11 terrorist at-tacks? Why did George Bush secretly sneak a plane full of Saudis out of America while all other planes were grounded? Why was Saudi Arabia's involvement in 9/11 kept secret? Did Saddam Hussein's re-fusal to accept US dollars for Iraqi oil inspire bipartisan American support to go to war with Iraq?[104] Many questions go beyond the scope of this book, but one fact is clear: The tension created by one country's privilege to "print energy" is quite evident.

AMERICAN COST-BENEFIT ANALYSIS

I've had it so good in this world, you know. The odds were fifty-to-one against me being born in the United States in 1930. I won the lottery the day I emerged from the womb by being in the United States instead of in some other country where my chances would have been way different.[105] —Warren Buffet, *The Snowball.*

Could America's benefits from the Black Gold Standard be achieved through something that costs less?

The Black Gold Standard provides at least three major benefits for Americans:

1. Increased global demand for US dollars.
2. Increased global demand for US debt.
3. Ability to buy oil with printed money.

Printing US dollars to fund deficit spending requires a methodical increase in the global demand for US dollars. Otherwise, the collapse of the Bretton Woods Gold Exchange Standard would have sparked hyperinflation and collapsed the US economy during the 1970s.

For over 50 years, the Black Gold Standard created synthetic demand for more US dollars to be printed. The <u>dollars-for-oil</u> system is simple. Foreign countries work hard to buy US dollars that are then used to purchase oil on the global market. Artificial demand for US dollars puts downward pressure on American inflation and upward pressure on foreign inflation as workers sell their native currencies to buy US dollars.

For this reason, the US dollar is the best fiat money in the world. If you go to a country plagued by hyperinflation, you will find most working people save in US dollars. US dollars may save people from hyperinflation in their native currencies, but it converts foreign workers into US taxpayers who pay the US inflation tax without the benefits of the US spending programs. This is how America exports inflation onto the world.

The impacts of this inflation-export scheme go far beyond offering foreign workers a deceptive savings tool. Foreign businesses face a big problem. It is expensive to trade their native currencies for US dollars on foreign exchange markets. To buy oil with US dollars and avoid expensive currency exchange fees, most overseas manufacturers will accept US dollars for their exports.

This financial incentive to avoid currency exchange fees creates a currency arbitrage opportunity that makes it nearly impossible for American companies to resist offshoring work that was once done by the American working class.

Billionaire Warren Buffet said being born an American is like winning the lottery. There is a financial advantage to living in the land of the world's money printer, but there is also an often-overlooked moral disadvantage: Consumerism.

The psychological effect of "buy now before inflation makes prices go up" has created a fiat flash-sale mindset that incites wasteful spending.

Americans have packed their antiques, basements, garages, and storage lockers full of cheap imported goods that are no longer useful in daily life. At the end of 2020, over 2 billion square feet of self-storage space was rentable in America.[106] This is the equivalent of 897,492 single-family homes.[107] With 580,466 homeless Americans, self-storage space alone could house 1.5 times the US homeless population.[108]

From mental illness to plastic pollution, the harm of an infinite money supply chasing finite earthly goods defies natural law. Fiat money cheapens hard work and punishes frugality. It has transformed Americans from creators into consumers. Fiat money has grown wealth inequality and reduced generosity. It forces you to tirelessly chase after money with an infinite denominator. To chase requires action, and actions speak louder than words. Our time, energy, and talents have shifted away from loving our neighbors to loving our complicated money.

Complicated money complicates politics. The main reason it is difficult to elect competent political leaders today is complexity. Most issues measured in fiat money are too complex to campaign on in a thoughtful way, so politicians descend into culture wars. It is important to recognize that politicians do not create culture; they reflect culture. Culture wars get people fired up. They create a false sense that your vote is "making a difference." Governments exist to help citizens protect their life, liberty, and property. Culture belongs to local communities.

Our civilization is quickly transitioning from the industrial age to the information age. If we allow money to lie about information, then a dark dystopian future awaits humanity. If we can constrain money with true information, then I'm optimistic we can build a better future.

Let's explore how Bitcoin can help unite a politically divided world.

ORANGE GOVERNMENT

A government for and by the people will use money that is created for and by the people.

If Americans desire freedom, we must revisit the ethics behind the creation of our currency. For a free market political system to thrive, rich and poor alike must know for certain what percentage of the total money supply they own today, tomorrow, and 100 years from now.

This type of transparency is not possible with gold, silver, or fiat money. Only Bitcoin can be a transparent, sustainable, predictable, and efficient system of digital money to fund a transparent, sustainable, predictable, and efficient political system.

You are now armed with ideas around how the invention of Bitcoin changes the future of money and economics. Next, let's unpack five of the most difficult political issues of our time, so we can imagine how Bitcoin changes the future of politics.

1) INFLATION

"I'd like either President Biden or President Trump to explain the lockdowns to us. That was a $16 trillion dollar mistake. We shifted $4 trillion dollars in wealth from the middle class in this country to the super rich, this new aristocracy of billionaires. The lockdowns created a new billionaire per day, 500 billionaires. And the people who came into the lockdown with a billion dollars increased their wealth by 30 percent. 41% of black-owned businesses will never reopen. Some of those businesses had two to three generations of sweat equity and currency in them. We closed 3.3 million businesses without due process and without just compensation. Both White Houses were collaborating with Amazon and social media to shut down their competitors. Amazon got to shut down 3.3 million competitors and we got a two-year lesson in how to do shopping on Amazon. And those retail businesses, the heart and soul of our economy, got shut down.[109]
— Robert F. Kennedy Jr., 2024 Democratic Presidential Candidate

Inflation is wealth redistribution.

Keynes was wrong. Printing money does not create wealth, it only redistributes wealth to people who are closer to the money printer.

If Americans desire to live in a free country, the authoritarian assault on working class wealth and individual liberties in response to the COVID-19 pandemic must become a lesson learned and not a lesson repeated. The US Constitution cannot be suspended when citizens need it the most.

There is a strong legal case that money supply inflation is an unconstitutional form of counterfeiting by politicians and bankers. Intentional inflation of the money supply is silent taxation without representation. It devalues the wages of workers to fund the loans of powerful people.

<u>US Constitution Article 1 Section 8 (Clauses 5-6)</u>: "*The Congress shall have the Power To ... coin Money, regulate the Value thereof, and of foreign Coin, and fix the Standard of Weights and Measures; To provide for the Punishment of counterfeiting the Securities and current Coin of the United States.*"[110]

Legally, the US Congress has surrendered their obligation to coin, regulate, and fix the value of American money. The Federal Reserve is permitted to bypass punishment for counterfeiting and debasing the American currency. This presidentially appointed and Senate-confirmed board of seven governors is permitted to feed newly printed US dollars into a network of private, for-profit banks. Each governor serves a 14-year term making politicians, who appoint governors to the Federal Reserve board, politically unaccountable to voters for the results.

The fiat system of new money creation prevents voters from holding elected representatives responsible at the ballot box for devaluing their money. In this way, intentional inflation is a sly and roundabout way of taxing the poor and draining economic energy from the working class.

<u>US Constitution Article 1 Section 10 (Clause 1)</u>: "*No State shall enter into any Treaty, Alliance, or Confederation; grant Letters of Marque and Reprisal; coin Money; emit Bills of Credit; make any Thing but gold and silver Coin a Tender in Payment of Debts...*"[111]

The opposite of freedom is forcing a poor man to work for money that a rich man can create for free. This is why the US constitution specifies gold and silver as the only suitable legal tender in the repayment of debts. US states cannot create paper money to repay debts without work.

Like gold and silver, creating new bitcoin requires physical work. Bitcoin miners use electricity and hardware to fuse physical power into digital money. Even the pseudonymous inventor of Bitcoin, Satoshi Nakamoto, paid for the electricity and hardware required to mine the first bitcoin.

Money is more than a tool; it reflects America's values and beliefs.

For this reason, you may join me in considering "In God We Trust" on American money to be a deceptive declaration. After America abandoned the gold standard, dollars became divorced from any divine constraint on the new supply of money. If God's laws of nature and physical scarcity do not control the dollar supply, then why do we still allow this pretend proclamation of faith to be printed on American money?

Bitcoin is an opportunity for America to embrace a commodity-based, divinely constrained money that tells the truth within a real economy.

How the US government can fix inflation:

- *Amend the US Constitution to uphold bitcoin financial privacy, self-custody, and mining rights.*
- *Promote peer-to-peer commerce by removing capital gains tax on Bitcoin transactions.*
- *Eliminate unit bias of whole bitcoin by talking about satoshis instead of whole coins (2.1 quadrillion units).*
- *Establish a 10-year transition plan to move from the Black Gold Standard to the bitcoin standard.*

2) CORRUPTION

"Democrats need to make it a top priority just to get rid of this debt ceiling. The Republicans have shown us enough times now how they plan to use it. And if we don't learn from that, shame on us."[112] —Elizabeth Warren, US Senator from Massachusetts.

Policymakers are drunk on debt, and it shows.

The fiat political cycle is predictable. Politicians buy votes with debt creation. Politicians make donors rich with debt creation. Voters get angry at politicians as new money from debt creation causes prices to rise faster than wages. Political problems get worse. Voters elect a new politician — the one who best entertains their attention and anger. The losing politician goes to work for the donors whom they helped make rich.

The root cause of most political corruption is simpler than you may think. Government budgets are supported by infinitely printable fiat money. An unnatural system of limitless money has transformed elections from friendly competitions to death matches over control of the money printer.

Printable budgets imprint a synthetic measure of economic value within government. Federal agencies are not required to abide by the laws of physics and therefore show no respect for scarcity. This synthetic economic reality for government spending enables ambitious politicians to promise tax cuts and government spending that are completely divorced from the reality of physical scarcity back here on Earth.

Fiat money allows politicians to become lazy in their problem-solving abilities. Why work hard to make peace and collaborate with your political enemies to solve hard problems when you can just print your way out of the problems? The path of least resistance in Washington, D.C., is to print new money. This system of broken political physics makes long-term devaluation of fiat currency a nearly 100% certainty.

How is the US government's printing of new money accomplished? Before we talk about the corrupt counterfeiting practice of quantitative easing (QE), you need to know that the reserve asset of the world is not really the dollar; it is government debt sold on the global bond market.

All government overspending is funded by selling government debt. What matters most is who buys the debt.

When government debt is sold to you, the US Treasury department uses your existing money to pay for government overspending. You agree to wait until a maturation date for repayment. In exchange for waiting, you bid to purchase the US Treasury bill, note, or bond at a discount of its matured value. The difference between the purchase price of this debt and its matured value is referred to as its yield to maturity.

When new government debt is sold to a commercial bank, QE enables the central bank to pledge to buy this debt from the commercial bank before it matures. In the shadows of the secondary bond market, ownership of existing government debt is transferred from the commercial bank to the central bank, and in exchange the central bank adds new digits to the cash balance of the commercial bank.

This sideways QE trade is how the Federal Reserve uses commercial banks to indirectly fund government overspending.

The subtle scheme gives **private** commercial banks **public** permission to scoop up obscene amounts of government debt. By acting as an eager bond buyer with a blank check, the Federal Reserve attempts to eliminate any private sector risk of "overbuying" government treasury bonds.

While the US Treasury does not directly print new money through the Federal Reserve to fund government overspending, it does achieve the same result by selling government debt to commercial banks who already know they are going to flip their debt purchases to the central bank.

Around the world, trillions of dollars in artificial government debt buying pressure from central banks kept interest rates artificially low throughout the global economy. Instead of letting bond yields rise when the supply of new government debt outpaced demand from the free market, central banks told commercial banks to go on bond-buying benders and their money printers would be there to pick up the tab.

From 2008 to 2022, the Federal Reserve printed $6 trillion new dollars to buy US Treasury bills, notes, and bonds on the secondary market.[113]

Since quantitative easing began in November 2008, the Federal Reserve has successfully manipulated bond markets to lower the cost of printing new money.[114] By making it cheap to fund government and commercial loans, the M2 money supply has nearly tripled since QE began.

In layman's terms, QE artificially lowered interest rates which gave banks an unnatural ability to flood our economy with trillions of new dollars.

Instead of the government selling debt to existing money within the bond market, the Federal Reserve printed new money to indirectly fund government overspending. The political hazard created by this centrally-planned artificial ceiling on bond yields cannot be overstated.

Unlike Prince John in Robin Hood, central bank-funded politicians no longer have to go door-to-door in Nottingham to beg for gold from the poor to collect taxes. To fund overspending – politicians, central bankers and commercial bankers have partnered to print away your savings.

Dollar devaluation may be a silent tax on the poor, but it is a loud asset inflation gift to rich political donors.

I used to wonder why anti-Wall Street politicians like Barack Obama or Elizabeth Warren would be paid enormous sums of money to speak at some of America's largest corporations.[115] Even socialist-leaning politicians who decry the evils of capitalism are flooded with a flurry of paid speeches, book deals, and K-street lobbying contracts from private corporations within the so-called "capitalist" system.[116]

It turns out, government overspending is a lucrative business for rich and powerful campaign donors.

The political power within a fiat system favors debt creators. This is due to the efficiency by which cheap debt creation sparks inflation, which transfers buying power away from the working class and toward the super-rich asset-holding class.

Only after you grasp inflation incentives within fiat politics can you grasp why American election spending has grown to such grotesque levels.

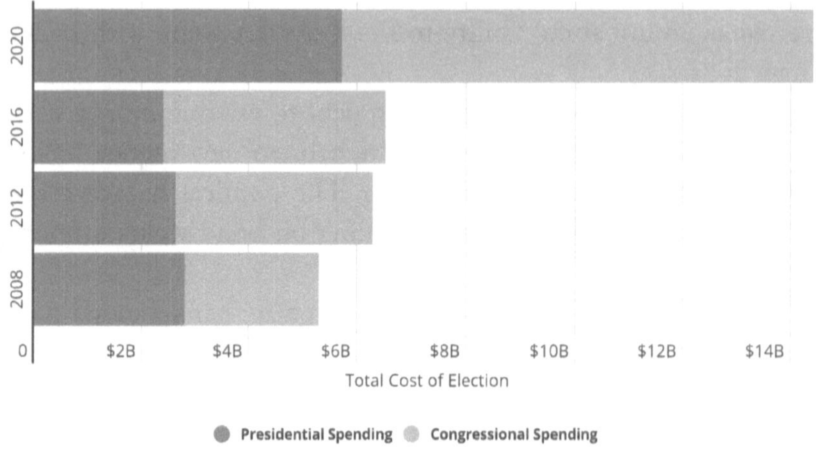

Souce: OpenSecrets.org[117]

The price of politics is wrong. Political donors driven by the allure of new fiat money, drove the price of the 2020 American election up to $14.4 billion. This was double the previously most expensive election in US history.[117] For context, the total GDP of Rwanda in 2020 was $13.2 billion dollars. Political campaigns wasted more on 2020 election advertising than the entire GDP of an African country with 13 million people.[118]

What is the cure for the sickening price tag of American politics? The right believes America is a free market where corporations should be allowed to make political donations. The left believes legislation can take the money out of politics. Instead of pretending centrally planned fiat money creates a free market or legislation can take money out of politics, a better option is to take politics out of the money.

If incentives drive behavior, then unprintable money will make bad politics expensive.

Since printing more bitcoin is not possible, politicians will not be tempted to use the Federal Reserve to print money instead of raising taxes.

When direct taxation for government spending is required, more transparency and accountability will be demanded from taxpayers. If a politician thinks a new war or a new welfare program is a good idea, they must make that case to voters, raise taxes, and measure results.

Unprintable bitcoin will allow voters to hold lawmakers accountable for spending their money. Bitcoin is a financial tool that empowers voters to objectively measure policy successes or failures over time. How will better money change voter sentiment towards politicians?

On a bitcoin standard, voters will be more sensitive to wasteful spending habits of political candidates. By adopting a bitcoin savings mindset, it will be a red flag in the minds of voters to see wasteful campaign spending. This frivolous fiat money behavior will be seen as a prelude to wasteful government spending and higher taxation. Within a fixed money system, an engaged and responsible electorate will naturally shift the incentives for wasteful campaign spending into lean, substantive political debates moderated on social media.

How can we know voters will adopt a savings mindset under a bitcoin standard? Human psychology. People are less likely to waste money that will be worth more in the future. If politics reflect culture, bitcoin can make frugal characteristics in politicians more attractive. Better incentives are how you decrease demand from mega-donors and remove their strings to corruptible politicians.

Big, visible, immovable property is a corruption magnet. A corrupt politician walks by a big building, looks at it, and thinks of creative ways to take it away from the undeserving rich person. The rich man asks himself, "Do I want my property taken away, or do I want to play the political game?" When the rich man plays the political game and realizes he can influence the politician to keep his property, he begins to try to influence the politician to take away the property of his competitors.

Unlike a building or a company, the rich man can move his bitcoin away from the corrupt politician to a more favorable jurisdiction instead of playing political games with taxation and regulation. Bitcoin is a little invisible movable property that deters corruption.

How Bitcoin reduces political corruption:

- *It reduces the cost of American elections by frugal voters favoring frugal candidates.*
- *It eliminates printable budgets so mega-donors do not get rich from government overspending.*
- *It encourages government spending transparency, accountability, and integrity by enacting a simple direct tax.*

3) DEBT

"I think the biggest threat we have to our national security is our debt."[119] —Admiral Mike Mullen, President Obama's Chairman of the Joint Chiefs of Staff.

If we follow the current growth in national debt, 6.5% annually between 2013 and 2023, by 2083 your grandchildren are on track to work in an economy that is suffocated by $1.5 quadrillion dollars of US government debt. The fiat debt dystopia that awaits your grandchildren would likely resemble a form of indentured servitude where future generations are forced to surrender their work to a class of politically connected debt creators.

Does a realistic deterrent to this dark future of debt slavery exist? Yes, the economy must switch from debt-based dollars to bitcoin.

As bitcoin adoption grows in America, the legal protections for citizens using the protocol also grows among lawmakers. The more politicians embrace the technological breakthrough of bitcoin, the faster economic laws can peacefully transition our economy to better money.

Legal tender laws and capital gains taxes are why most people save bitcoin and spend dollars today.

When legal tender laws and capital gains taxes are lifted, **Thiers' law** suggests that businesses will stop accepting bad money and demand to be paid in good money.[120] You will know the economic transition from debt-based money to bitcoin is nearly complete when businesses demand payment in unprintable bitcoin instead of printable dollars.

While we do not know the day and hour of Thiers' transition from bad money to good money, the math of America's national debt does give us a clue that its arrival is near. The American national debt is on track to surpass 500% of GDP this century. Apart from the money printer at the Federal Reserve, who will buy this unpayable debt and what yield will these buyers expect for their investment?

The Fed cannot save fiat money. Fiat history is littered with countries who were forced to rapidly devalue their currencies to pay high yields to bondholders. When fiat money collapses under the weight of unpayable debt, economic chaos, poverty, and violent revolutions are sparked. Rather than falling victim to a debt spiral, America should plan for a "Monetary Manhattan Project" that resets its unpayable debt into bitcoin.

Wargame #1: US National Debt without Bitcoin

The US government builds a central bank digital currency (CBDC) in secret. Technology rails developed by initiatives like the "Hamilton Project" and the New York Federal Reserve turn on during the next global crisis.[121] Private retail banks are cut out of the monetary system. The Federal Reserve is depicted as spineless bureaucrats who lacked the tools and risk management regulations to properly regulate greedy bankers.

An army of CBDC advocates within the US Treasury tout cost savings, system stability, universal basic income (UBI), and tax simplification as major benefits of switching to a government-backed digital currency. Under the weight of a global crisis, the uninformed masses succumb to fear tactics and are given stimulus to use the CBDC. Financial privacy safeguards are promised to overcome the opinions of liberty-loving critics.

Expiration dates are placed on physical cash. Early CBDC converts are given bonuses in their CBDC wallets. These bonuses dilute the money of late CBDC adopters. Under the guise of government-backed blockchain, Americans are fooled into believing the CBDC is better than Bitcoin.

Foreign nations see CBDC debasement necessary to fund US government overspending. Foreign nations flee into bitcoin. CBDC deposits begin to flee into bitcoin as well. Bitcoin is blamed for the CBDC system going up in flames. To stabilize the financial system, the US government outlaws bitcoin purchases using its CBDC.

The CBDC is a programmable digital currency, so numerous other banned transaction types follow the Bitcoin ban. Carbon emissions, dietary decisions, religious affiliations, and political protests are all punishable by turning off your CBDC wallet. Saving is labeled as hoarding. One-year expiration dates are enforced on the balance in each citizen's digital wallet. If you do not use the money, you lose the money.

Savings are outlawed under the banner of economic stimulation. Without the ability to save, the working class must work longer and harder to keep up with the expansion in the total supply of the CBDC. Eventually, the working class rises up against the oppression of the digital money printers and a violent revolution ensues. Millions of lives are lost to a revolutionary war for economic liberty.

Wargame #2: US National Debt with Bitcoin

The US government builds a Strategic Bitcoin Reserve (SBR) in secret to accumulate bitcoin at the lowest possible price in US dollars. Since bitcoin is absolutely scarce and stores less than 1% of global wealth in 2023, the US government is able to nefariously manipulate markets with large buy and sell orders.

The US Treasury uses low liquidity within the bitcoin market to create high volatility. By strategically buying and selling large quantities of bitcoin across small wallets, they create high volatility and scare away working-class investors, who remain unaware and uneducated on the technology.

The US government acquires the largest amount of bitcoin possible before the great debt reset.

Once the US SBR has acquired an adequate amount of bitcoin to secure the national debt, the US President announces details about the American SBR program. Global demand for debt denominated in US dollars falls and bitcoin is hit with a flood of global demand fighting over its finite supply. The value of US national debt falls as the US dollar plummets, and the value of the US SBR skyrockets overnight.

The US Congress approves a conversion window to allow US dollars and US Treasury bondholders to convert their holdings into bitcoin at a fixed rate. Think of this as the inverse of FDR's Gold Exchange Act of 1934. Instead of confiscating gold, trapping citizens in fiat banks and then devaluing US dollars by 41%, this is an act of financial liberation. Bitcoin distribution to US citizens reverses the theft of FDR's Great Steal.

There is no need for an economics degree to recognize the fiscal path of America is unsustainable. America cannot cut its way out of debt; it can't tax its way out of debt. As the interest expense on the US national debt increases, default becomes more likely. The global bond market will continue to demand higher interest rates to hold American debt. Extraordinary and unpredictable growth in interest payments on the US national debt will continue to eat away at economic productivity until Americans embrace bitcoin.

How Bitcoin can peacefully resolve US national debt:

- *Build a Strategic Bitcoin Reserve.*
- *Redenominate US national debt into bitcoin to devalue past debt and pay off bondholders from the SBR.*
- *Reverse FDR's Great Steal and convert existing US dollars into bitcoin at an exchange rate approved by US Congress.*

4) WAR

When questioned why Parliament had lost respect among the people of the Colonies, Benjamin Franklin answered:

"To a concurrence of causes: the restraints lately laid on their trade, by which the bringing of foreign gold and silver into the Colonies was prevented; **the prohibition of making paper money among themselves***, and then demanding a new and heavy tax by stamps; taking away, at the same time, trials by juries, and refusing to receive and hear their humble petitions."*[122] British Parliament in February 1766.

Who gets the right to manipulate paper money? That's a question that has instigated more wars than any other.

America's founding fathers saw the Currency Act of 1764 as King George III's attempt to take control of the 13 colonial monetary systems.[123] The colonists wanted to print and control their own paper money, while the Crown wanted the colonists to use the British pound. Both sides manipulated money, but who reserved the right to manipulate the paper money became hotly contested. Money printing privilege is an often overlooked, yet a major grievance that led to the American Revolution and Declaration of Independence.

Historically speaking, paper backed by gold and paper fiat money has prolonged war. When taxed directly for war, taxpayers run out of patience for war campaigns. When money is limited to pay for more soldiers and weapons, governments are more motivated to make peace.

In 1913, the Federal Reserve began splitting money from reality. War is now less expensive in paper money and more expensive in human lives.

Since the founding of the Federal Reserve, America has lost 623,973 lives to foreign wars across the globe.[124] Global wars are estimated to have caused 85 million military and civilian deaths since 1913.[125] Over the last century, the death caused by global war has been horrific.[126] Yet this staggering death toll barely scratches the surface on the deeper destruction fiat-funded wars have inflicted on our culture.

As the grandson of World War II, Korean, and Vietnam veterans, I saw first-hand the damage of post-war PTSD — or post-traumatic stress disorder — within my family. Divorce, abandonment, suicide, homelessness, and substance abuse are silent killers within our veteran communities. It is worth asking whether unprintable money, like bitcoin, could have shortened the suffering caused by a century of prolonged fiat-funded wars.

- If the German, Italian, and Japanese soldiers refused to be paid in fiat money, would World War II have ended sooner?
- If the gold standard was enforceable, would Lyndon B. Johnson and Richard Nixon have approached the Vietnam War differently?
- If bitcoin was the global reserve asset instead of US Treasuries, would George W. Bush have handled the War on Terror differently?

To evade the great expense of human lives, money must make war as expensive as possible.

If you want a more peaceful world to exist in the future, you must rethink the permissions you grant to warmongers by paying the silent inflation tax. If war taxes are taken directly instead of through fiat money printing, future wars may be mitigated or avoided altogether. Bound by the unprintable nature of bitcoin, negative taxpayer sentiment may deter politicians from escalating war beyond bitcoin war tax revenues.

Throughout history, immobile sovereign wealth like gold, real estate, and energy infrastructure has encouraged warmongers to invade weaker countries. The prospect of killing a foreign people to steal their wealth has been an irresistible temptation for countless tyrants. How does the incentive for invasion change after the majority of a nation's wealth is stored in cyberspace? Without a weaker nation surrendering its multisignature private keys, a hostile invader will no longer be able to kill, steal, and destroy to confiscate bitcoin.

It may be hopeful speculation to imagine how unprintable money might make the world a more peaceful place. Hope boils down to optimism about the future. Without hope, fear of the future becomes a temptation to surrender your liberty for a false sense of security. Freedom is not free — nor is it comfortable. To escape the theft of one man claiming rights to the fruits of your labor, there has always been a price to pay.

Learning from history is the best price we can pay for freedom. To postpone World War III, let's revisit what led to World War II.

In retaliation for the Japanese invasion of China, on July 26, 1941, American president Franklin D. Roosevelt seized all Japanese assets in the United States.[127] The pain inflicted by financial sanctions gave the Japanese government the green light it needed from its taxpayers to attack America.[128] 134 days later, Japan attacked America in Pearl Harbor, Hawaii. The next day, America entered World War II.[129]

In retaliation for the 2022 Russian invasion of Ukraine, American president Joe Biden went one step further than FDR. The Biden administration seized all Russian government assets in the United States, froze hundreds of billions of dollar reserves belonging to the Russian Central Bank reserves, and restricted the access of Russian banks to SWIFT — the dominant system for global financial transactions.[130] The financial war waged against Russia has sent a clear message to the rest of the world: If the United States government does not like what you are doing, it will freeze or seize your money.

History does not repeat itself, but it always rhymes. Answering the ethical questions surrounding whether or not FDR should have retaliated against Japan or whether or not the G7 nations should have retaliated against Russia is beyond the scope of this book.

I want you to think about how the weaponization of the US dollar has weakened it as the global reserve currency. No longer can America's friends and foes responsibly trust the US dollar or US Treasury bond as neutral global reserve assets. Moving forward, every dollar-denominated financial instrument will retain its value only if its holder retains political favor from the United States government.

BRICS nations (Brazil, Russia, India, China, and South Africa) are publicly plotting to dethrone the US dollar hegemony. Whether BRICS dethrones the US dollar first or bitcoin does, the pain on American households could be sudden and severe. In 2021, the US dollar accounted for 60% of international reserves. Overnight, a flood of foreign US debt holders could sell $7 trillion dollars' worth of Treasury bonds and a flood of international reserves could be sold back into the American economy.[131] Hyperinflation is America's Achilles heel.

Debt is a weapon of war. Debt-based money instigates, propagates, and prolongs war. Bitcoin can be a tool for peacemakers.

How Bitcoin can deter wars:

- *Encourage bitcoin self-custody to mitigate the risk of bitcoin-backed paper money being used to fund endless wars.*
- *Amend the US constitution to require Congress to vote quarterly on direct war taxation rates.*
- *Support the use of bitcoin as a neutral global reserve currency to invalidate the propaganda of warmongering dictators.*

5) IMMIGRATION

"You know, 11 million people live in the shadows. I believe they're already American citizens."[132] —Joe Biden, US Vice President, 2014

Poor people are paying cartels to be smuggled closer to the world's money printer.

I used to think that illegal immigration was a black-and-white issue. If your first act in America is to break the law by cutting the line, then you should move to the back of line. I still believe in secure borders and rule of law, however, after learning about America's exportation of inflation onto Latin America, I now believe it is more of a nuanced issue than I previously thought.

Most migrants do not want to leave their homeland, but printable money is a mighty magnet that pulls the world's poor away from their family and friends. Latin men are leaving their families to work in America and destroying the previously strong Latin American family unit.

If you visit the countries from which people flee, you will notice a common problem. Latin American countries like Venezuela, Argentina, Haiti, Chile, Cuba, and Nicaragua all suffer from regular bouts of hyperinflation. For this reason, most local workers save in US dollars.

As the most stable of all fiat currencies, the US dollar has been exported by America into weaker countries around the globe. The systematic exportation of inflation has silently transformed a majority of the world's poor into US taxpayers. Maybe this is why Joe Biden thinks of undocumented workers living in the shadows as already being American citizens. By this standard, American citizenship means nothing.

If you think about America's inflation export from an ethical perspective, it will most likely change how you view the illegal immigration problem and its proposed solutions. Unlike foreign workers, American citizens benefit from printing more dollars to fund government overspending on welfare programs, military protection, and housing subsidies.

When you consider new dollars are created with new debt creation based on citizenship, the subliminal incentives of immigrants to illegally cross the US border to work in America becomes clearer. Your location and citizenship determine whether or not you get to mine new dollars without physical work requirements.

Hopefully you are beginning to see the injustice facing foreign workers. Weaker local fiat currencies are forcing foreign workers to save in US dollars, and they silently pay America's inflation tax without any of the US government benefits.

In Chapter 1, we learned that an unsolved problem in the fiat system is more profitable than a solved one. There is no better example of the broken incentive caused by broken money than the US immigration system. For decades, all political parties have exploited it.

Instead of asking what motivates desperate migrants to pay drug cartels to illegally cross the US border, greed has motivated the Keynesian Kings to fill America's legal immigration system with unbearable wait times and bottlenecks. The result of incentivized inaction is a bureaucratic quagmire where the cost-benefit analysis facing migrants has been tilted to favor illegal activity.

In fiat politics, emotional wedge issues funnel more fiat money into politics. Most Democrats blame Republican racism as to why undocumented immigrants are denied legal status in the United States. Most Republicans blame Democrat exploitation as to why national security and fiscal responsibility are being neglected by open border policies. Regardless of your politics, the humanitarian crisis caused by broken incentives within the American immigration system is undeniably tragic.

US Customs and Border patrol set a new record of over 2.7 million migrant border crossings in FY 2022.[133] That means more migrants crossed the US Southern border in one year than the entire population of New Mexico. That same year, the number of "got-aways," those who successfully sneaked across the border without being encountered, could have been over 500,000 persons.[134]

Statistically, it makes no sense that 500,000 got-aways illegally crossed the US border to work in America. America's enemies are most assuredly exploiting America's open borders for nefarious purposes. Drug cartels are being enriched; big corporations are being enriched; open border politicians are being enriched. And ultimately, the wages of illegal immigrants are being exploited to hide inflation.

If Americans are unwilling to do the jobs done by immigrants, then why don't we pay Americans more money to do those jobs and let prices rise? This is more ethical than exploiting the labor of poor migrant workers who are forced to live and work in the shadows of our society.

To keep the debt money solvent, the Keynesian Kings need economic proof-of-work energy in form of cheap labor. Immigrant labor creates demand for dollars without requiring government spending on citizenship. Labor exploitation keeps the fiat machine solvent.

Illegal immigration is plagued by broken incentives. Debt-based money incentivizes illegal activity. Bitcoin can be a tool that allows immigrants to remain at home with their families and prosper economically in their homeland.

How Bitcoin can reduce illegal immigration:

- *Secure all US borders to dispel the global notion that America has an open border.*
- *Open up legal immigration to lower the cost and speed up the deadlines for decisions.*
- *End the practice of inflation exportation by embracing a politically neutral global bitcoin standard.*

LIGHTNING ROUND

How can Bitcoin make other important political issues better?

- HEALTHCARE
  - A strict and transparent bitcoin budget for federal agencies like the FDA and CDC will increase accountability.
  - Equal access to money will increase competition among local hospital systems.
  - Peer-to-peer money will inspire peer-to-peer healthcare networks that bypass bureaucratic middlemen.
  - Less administration costs to comply with bureaucracy will increase the pay of healthcare providers.
  - Truth in money can restore truth in food to combat the obesity epidemic which is driving up healthcare costs.

- EDUCATION
  - Educate children on new creative fields of study instead of fiat-funded, brainless, administrative work.
  - Lower cost of living to give more parents the financial ability to homeschool or private-school their children.
  - Allow technology, apprenticeships, and skills-testing to replace debt-fueled college educations.

- o Encourage widespread financial education about the differences between fiat money and bitcoin.
- o Encourage businesses to hire based on candidate character and potential to train their new employees.

- **CRIME**
  - o Deter crime by shifting society to a savings mindset and people will consider the long-term consequences of their actions.
  - o Rebuild trust between police departments and minority communities with financial transparency.
  - o Grow the wealth of the poor and working class to reduce financial stress in order to lower rates of divorce and father absenteeism.
  - o Reduce substance abuse by replacing the hopelessness of fiat poverty with hope for a more prosperous future.
  - o Motivate idle youth to do honest work by teaching them to save money that grows in value over time.

- **ENVIRONMENT**
  - o Restore environmental order by using limited money for a limited supply of Earth's natural resources.
  - o Mining bitcoin makes renewable energy generation, storage, and transfer more affordable and reliable than fossil fuels.
  - o Reduce flare gas and methane emissions by selling wasted energy to mobile bitcoin mining rigs.
  - o Sell stranded renewable power to fund renewable energy research before bringing it onto the power grid.
  - o Strengthen power grids by enlisting Bitcoin miners to buy up excess electricity supply through demand load balancing.

- PRIVACY

  - Limit government control by using money that is beyond government control.
  - Avoid digital prisons for the politically incorrect by supporting pseudonymous neutral money that assumes innocence.
  - Teach children proper self-custody of bitcoin private keys in schools.
  - Make it easy and accessible for anyone to run a Bitcoin node and Lightning payment channels.
  - Regulate law enforcement to catch a criminal before devoting any resources to snoop through Bitcoin transactions.

CONCLUSION

"Paper money has had the effect in your State that it ever will have, to ruin commerce, oppress the honest, and open a door to every species of fraud and injustice."[135] —George Washington to Thomas Jefferson on August 1, 1786.

"Paper is poverty. It is only the ghost of money, not money itself... abuses are also inevitable and, by breaking up the measure of value, make a lottery of all private property."[136] —Thomas Jefferson.

If paper money is poverty, will Americans have enough bitcoin to run a peaceful government?

Unlike the failed gold standard, a global bitcoin standard will require complete government transparency to function properly. No longer will the US Treasury be allowed to fake reserve audits like it did under the golden guise of secret security at Fort Knox.[137]

At regular intervals, taxpayers and foreign governments will expect every nation to prove ownership of the private keys associated with the government's public Bitcoin addresses. There will most likely be a multisignature system of checks and balances where 75% of leadership, government agencies, and congressional committees are required to sign with their private keys to prove ownership during these audits.

Regardless of the methodology, a radically new incentive for all nation-states to flex their bitcoin reserves has the potential to change global politics for the better. When you combine the transparency of Bitcoin and the game theory behind an absolutely scarce supply of money, you are left with one vital question for national security: Will Americans have enough bitcoin to run a peaceful government?

Scarcity serves as the bedrock of economics. Your time and resources on Earth are scarce, and with bitcoin, your money can be scarce as well. Satoshi's discovery of verifiable digital scarcity was like the creation of a new board game in global politics. Within this new board game, the first nations to store their work in bitcoin benefit from the work of nations who postpone storing their work in bitcoin. Over time, this type of game theory, based on scarcity, punishes authoritarians who reject bitcoin by depriving them of future purchasing power.

Before we move on from this point, I feel it is necessary to reiterate the significance of this new technology. Whether you call bitcoin a currency or a commodity is irrelevant; never before has anything on Earth been transparently, verifiably, and unconditionally limited in supply.

We all know scarcity exists on Earth, but Bitcoin is the first technology to put a hard cap on this fundamental economic concept. For millennia, mankind has observed and estimated scarcity when choosing hard money that was difficult to break. However, as soon as a scarce commodity became used as money, a mix of corruption and innovation always led to producers finding ways to create more of it, which diluted its value.

If oil prices go up, oil producers innovate and find new ways to drill for more oil. If gold prices go up, gold miners innovate and find new ways to mine for more gold. If the value of the dollar goes up, the Federal Reserve lowers interest rates to increase the supply of dollars.

Bitcoin is different. No matter what the price of bitcoin climbs to in the future, no nation can mine for more bitcoin beyond the supply cap of 21 million. The American government could capture all of the mining power in the world, but they still would not control Bitcoin.

How can a government control Bitcoin?

According to author Mattew Fraser, Joseph Goebbels (Adolf Hitler's minister for public enlightenment and propaganda) said that, *"Propaganda works best when those who are being manipulated are confident, they are acting on their own free will."*[138]

The only way a government controls Bitcoin is by changing how we think about money. Like all forms of money, Bitcoin is an idea. The more people who store their work in this idea, the more valuable the money becomes. This is why Bitcoin has such an enthusiastic user base. The more people who get behind the idea of Bitcoin, the more powerful the network becomes. It is like a freedom virus of the mind. With each new person who saves their work in bitcoin, the government loses a little more control over each of our life savings.

A proverb in the Bitcoin community is "fix the money, fix the world."

Apolitical digital money may be the most significant political disruption in human history, yet most of the problems we face today cannot be fixed directly by bitcoin. Bitcoin is a bridge to a better world, not a guarantee of it. There are plenty of examples in the "cryptocurrency industry" where corrupt individuals have ridden the coattails of Bitcoin hype for fraudulent purposes. No matter what monetary system exists, political corruption will always exist. What Bitcoin does fix is transparency: It sets clear boundaries and limits on the power to subjugate the weak.

In a world where no politician can censor or counterfeit their way to wealth and power, the weakest in society are given a fair shot to make their mark on the world. If you can still buy unprintable bitcoin with printed money, you are early to this civil rights movement. One day, all wealth will require honest work. Honest work to earn bitcoin will sow the seeds for political freedom by incentivizing more making and less taking.

One litmus test for political freedom is whether you can leave your country with your wealth and without asking political permission to do so.

Early America thrived because the decentralization of US states allowed people to easily cross state borders to escape oppressive mayors and governors. Governments can collect taxes best on things that don't move. Physical real estate is an ideal tax target for governments because you can't move it. When property rights are mobile and password protected, politicians will be compelled to show more respect for taxpayers.

Most property today requires political permission to hold. If Bitcoin continues to swallow up the market share of all politically permissioned properties, then we reverse the relationship between individuals and government. All future permission will be sought from the individual.

I hope this chapter inspires you to think about what sort of country you want to leave for your loved ones. If you feel that unpayable debt is unacceptable, then I encourage you to peacefully protest by saving bitcoin. We need to elect leaders who are willing to follow the example of America's first President, George Washington. Like how Washington humbly refused to be king, we need to elect political leaders who are brave enough to turn off the fiat money printer. If not, our children will pay a high price for our illusion of money today.

Since 1800, 50 out of 52 countries who have reached a 130% debt-to-GDP ratio have defaulted. For now, the only two exceptions in history are present-day Japan and the United States of America. Bitcoin does not need America. To avoid death by debt, America needs Bitcoin.

Next, we wargame how property can be stolen from you to better understand why Bitcoin is better property.

4

PROPERTY

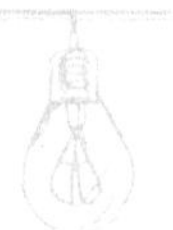

What is property? Property is an idea. Abraham Lincoln articulated it beautifully in this way, "Property is the fruit of labor."[140]

Property can be physical — like a home or vehicle — or nonphysical, like intellectual property, stock shares, money, or paid time off. While property takes many different forms, it is best understood to be something in your possession with ownership recognized by your government.

Therein lies the problem. The idea of property is not flawed; the laws to defend property are flawed. You only own property which can be defended. While you may be unable to recall a violent altercation where you successfully defended your property, it happens every day.

Globally, the military uses violence to deter foreign invaders from taking your property as the spoils of war. Locally, the police use violence and incarceration to deter criminals from taking your property. Most lawyers say possession is nine-tenths of the law. While this

115

saying may be true, it is the last one-tenth of the law that really determines who owns what: Recognition of ownership by the government.

Since the beginning of time, humans have been fighting over physical property. If you step outside of your front door and look down, the dirt below your feet has been violently fought over dozens of times throughout human history. Whether it's war between the Comanche tribe and the Apache tribe[141], or war between the Comanche tribe and the Americans, or war between the Americans and the British, or war between the Union and the Confederates, the use of violence to secure physical property rights has been a perpetual cycle of war.

If physical property rights require war, is replacing private ownership with some type of state-run communism better? No. Forcing charity through the state removes individual free will from society. Without the free will to transact, authentic love and genuine service becomes scarce. Look no further for a rejection of communism than the reliance on private property found in the Ten Commandments:

VIII: Thou shalt not steal.
X: Thou shalt not covet.

Whether you call it natural law or divine law, it is a self-evident truth that everyone is born with a civil right to not be stolen from.

If you live in a country with enforceable property rights laws, you are in the global minority. According to a 2020 Frontier Centre for Public Policy study, over 5.3 billion people live in a country with an International Property Rights Index ("IPRI") below 7.4.[142] (For context, the United States scored 8.05 and China scored 6.04 on this IPRI scale.) Cultures and customs may differ, but human nature is the same around the globe: No matter where you live, theft is wrong.

This 2020 study shows most of the global population is forbidden from keeping the fruits of their labor. Most governments hostilely and openly take the peoples' property by force. After learning about fiat money and how inflation is designed to steal your savings over time, do you think being stolen from openly or secretly is worse?

Why would anyone ever want to save fiat money? The flaws of fiat money makes saving money irrational. Fiat forces you to invest your savings into scarcer assets which will hopefully hold their value against freshly printed dollars.

Perhaps by design, fiat money is the ultimate economic distraction. Instead of mastering your craft as a doctor, lawyer, engineer, or tradesman, fiat forces you to compete with the Keynesian Kings in their game of investments. Armed with algorithms and insider information, it is like you are running on a treadmill beside Usain Bolt and Usain gets to turn up the speed on your treadmill whenever you start to get ahead.

Fiat money is why America has such a burned out and exhausted workforce.

As long as you choose to play the fiat money game, your productivity gains will be stolen by those who print the money. If you ignore Bitcoin, you are accepting your fate as the loser in this fiat money game and agree to always work harder to afford higher prices caused by inflation.

As a reminder from chapter 2, technology should be decreasing your cost of living, but the Keynesian Kings are printing new fiat money faster than the rate of innovation can reduce prices. If invited, would you join the Keynesian Kings' counterfeiting operation?

Under the pressure of dollar devaluation, many people are persuaded to drive getaway cars for these currency counterfeiters. An essential utility has been transformed into a money printing machine for the working class. Homeownership is an illusion of ownership designed to keep you asleep during the destruction of your dollars. Now it is time to reveal the not-so secret scheme to make you an accomplice counterfeiter.

THE COUNTERFEITED UTILITY

Merriam-Webster defines utility as something useful or designed for use.[143]

Air, food, water, clothing, and shelter are all essential utilities. Each of these utilities are biological requirements for human survival. As caring members of our communities, why shouldn't we all be working to make essential utilities as affordable as possible for everyone?

More affordable utilities may sound good, but what if it strikes a little closer to home? What if the price of your home dropped over time?

If you own a home, your instinctual reaction is panic. Your imagination is most likely flooded with financial terror. Your brain is bombed with thoughts of an underwater mortgage, foreclosure, and bankruptcy. On the contrary, if you rent a home, you happily welcome a drop in your rent payment. If a mortgage was like renting a home from the bank and your mortgage payments dropped over time, would you feel differently?

The truth is, since the invention of Bitcoin, real estate prices have been dropping in bitcoin terms. It does not matter how you and I feel about monetary value trending away from real estate and towards bitcoin, it is happening for one logical reason: Real estate is bad money.

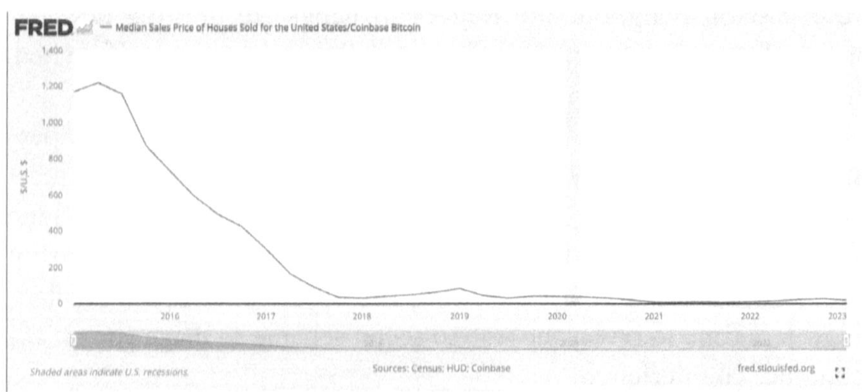

Source: FRED.[144]

Owning real estate is useful property designed to give us food and shelter, but it is not divisible, portable, durable, or uniform. This is why real estate is bad money and thus, despite popular opinion, owning real estate is not a reliable savings account for the working class.

Over the last 50 years, fiat money has cratered in value compared to real estate. After Nixon de-pegged the US dollar from gold, the new supply of real estate has been much lower than the new supply of US dollars coming onto the market. A half-century of scarcity imbalance between the creation of new dollars and the creation of new real estate has created unnatural growth in the value of real estate in terms of dollar prices. Unnatural fiat money has created the mirage of working-class wealth and misled many working people to believe real estate is a safe and reliable savings account.

If you are a well-behaved member of the working class, you are invited to save yourself from inflation by joining the counterfeiting club. Under the guise of affordable housing, the Keynesian Kings grant you permission to take out a mortgage and print new money from nothing. By purchasing unprintable real estate with freshly printed fiat money, millions of Americans join in on the counterfeiting game.

This debt deal with the Keynesian Kings to partake in unnatural money creation has caused working-class wages to not keep up with rising real estate prices. Down payments requirements are trending toward zero, and mortgage creation is trending towards pure money printing. This causes bidding wars on homes to become detached from economic reality.

The American dream of owning a home has become a nightmare for young people entering the workforce. Renting instead of securing a lifetime's worth of debt on an unaffordable home may seem like a punishment, but after bitcoin, avoiding unpayable debt may be a blessing in disguise. Bitcoin gives you the option to save up for a home instead of partaking in the Keynesian Kings' counterfeiting operation.

If you dig beyond your realtor's talking points about the financial benefits of home ownership, you'll notice that your deposit requirements and lending costs are much higher than the deposit requirements and the funding rates paid by Keynesian Kings. Also, you must work to pay back debt dollars that they created for free. But hey, at least you get to counterfeit fiat money *with* them.

Do you see an ethics problem here? By exploiting Americans' financial ignorance about money, an unaware working class has been lured into its role as a second-rate sidekick in the world's largest counterfeiting operation. As a useful Keynesian King accomplice, your mortgage down payment is between 0% and 20%, and you pretend there is a real depositor on the other side of your loan who is willing to lose money to fiat inflation of 6.9% for 30 years. The truth is American mortgages print new money and dilute the purchasing power of every dollar holder around the world.

If we want to renounce our role in the systemic theft of the poor by counterfeiting fiat money, we must allow the free market to dictate interest rates, not central banks. There should always be a real lender and a real borrower on both sides of every loan. We must let go of real estate being an investment and allow shelter to become an essential utility that gets more affordable over time.

Did you know a 30-year fixed rate mortgage is an exclusive privilege for Americans? As an example, in Canada, interest rates for mortgages have a renewal rate that adjusts every three to five years. Instead of locking in a fixed interest rate below inflation for 30 years, the rest of the world must suffer the consequences of erratic interest rate cycles. In the land of the world's money printer, the privilege of a fixed rate mortgage gives Americans an unfair advantage. This passport privilege to print new money creates envy, conflict, and price confusion around the world.

It is commonly said that human intelligence is essentially systematic error correction. If this is true, then printing new fiat money to buy real estate inevitably distorts our ability to intelligently value property. Fiat money adds many layers of complexity to purchasing decisions. Instead of considering the simple utility of a property, fiat money forces you to speculate on what a group of central bankers will do to the supply of money over the next month, next year, next decade, and next century.

When your money supply is unknown, long-term investments into utilities to save your money makes the most sense. You are betting on new debt creation and money supply expansion growing faster than the supply of utilities. America's requirement to make interest payments on an unpayable national debt makes betting on fiat money supply expanding faster than utilities a near mathematical certainty.

When the money supply is known, long-term investments into utilities no longer make sense. With a known money supply like bitcoin, investing in utilities is betting that future technology will fail to bring more and better supplies to market. This is like betting against the invisible hand of the free market. If a business cannot bring better products to market that save people time or money, it should fail.

Do you see the contrast? Fiat money relies on a pessimistic investment strategy where living gets more expensive over time. Bitcoin relies on an optimistic investment strategy, where living gets more affordable over time.

It goes without saying, money supply expansion is not the only way to value properties. Future factors such as local economics, government, and environment will all play their part in the supply-and-demand formula determining prices within the free market. The main point here is that bitcoin has a known money supply that allows us to value property without the complexities that come from an unknown — and unstable — money supply.

What would happen to prices if people printed new money to buy other utilities like food, water, and clothing?

If people printed money for food, water, and clothing, then those prices would go up. When money supply is created without work, power in society shifts away from hard work and toward the privileged few with the best access to the money printer who bid up the prices of utilities.

Shelter is no different than other utilities. If the working class chooses to monetize bitcoin as a savings account, then shelter will be demonetized and instead treated as a life-essential utility. Under the fiat system, real estate has become much more scarce than dollars. This scarcity imbalance has resulted in housing being hoarded by investors and saved as a money substitute by the working class.

Shelter will always be scarce, but bitcoin is verifiably more scarce than real estate. When you divide the most popular real estate investments on Earth by the maximum total supply of 21 million bitcoin, you clearly see that the scarcity advantage of good money tilts in favor of bitcoin:

- 109 homes[145] on Earth per 1 bitcoin.
- 1,247 acres of habitable land[146] on Earth per 1 bitcoin.

THE PROPERTY PARADIGM SHIFT

Physical property is a costly way to save money.

Real estate investor:

"I can live in my rental house. Good luck trying to live in your bitcoin!"

Bitcoin saver:

"My bitcoin can live in my head. Good luck getting a rental house to live in your head!"

Beyond the banter, this type of thinking exposes the grip of fiat indoctrination on the working class.

In the future, archeologists may look back at real estate and see it as an archaic ledger of people's wealth. Children will ask their teachers, "Why did people live inside their money?" I imagine teachers will respond with something like, "Before bitcoin, the world was a strange place."

Bitcoin's biggest hurdle is that most blue-collar workers want to see, touch, and taste their money. Despite quietly adapting to the convenience of digital dollars in their bank accounts and digital shares of stock in their retirement accounts, the concept of bitcoin as digital money is still seen as inferior compared to physical real estate, gold coins, or even green paper notes.

Why does digital bias exist? First things first. All honest gold bugs and landlords first have to admit it is impossible for a digital economy to run on physical money. If people continue to buy and sell more things online, then the only way to securely transfer value across the internet is with secure digital money. The question is not whether the future of money will be physical or digital, it is whether it is better for governments to control the rules of digital money or a decentralized group of strangers across the world to control the rules of digital money.

If you are still struggling with the concept of digital money being a better savings account than physical property, consider this perspective. No one really wants to own money; people want their money to buy stuff. This is why we all quietly transitioned from physical money stored in bank vaults to digits of money displayed on mobile banking apps. If bitcoin buys more stuff in the future, then no one will care that it is digital.

If the future of digital commerce is not saving physical property, but saving better money, then let's talk about our options:

Fiat Money 2.0: What if lawmakers passed a balanced budget amendment and tethered fiat money to a basket of physical commodities?

The fiat system is inherently backed by debt. No government has proven itself capable of resisting the temptation to overspend beyond tax revenues and print new fiat money to make up the difference. Since all bitcoin has been mined into existence by computers, it does not require debt to move throughout the economy. Proverbs 22:7 warns us, the borrower is the slave to the lender. In the spirit of freedom, poor slaves will revolt against their rich lenders. To promote peace among rich and poor people, debt money must be shattered into a thousand pieces.

Gold Standard 2.0: What if we revived the gold standard and built a verification system built on top of blockchain technology?

The physical nature of gold means you will always have to trust a human custodian to not issue more gold notes than physical gold held in its vault. When tracking any external physical item, blockchain technology does not remove the liability of human corruptibility. This is an important concept; if necessary, please reread that sentence. No matter what new marketing label is thrown on gold, it is ignorant to expect another round of trust in gold reserves to have a different outcome than that of Bretton Woods and Nixon's golden default. Never before in monetary history has one money standard been abandoned only to later be successfully reinstated. Gold is an old idea that doesn't work.

Bitcoin Standard: What if Bitcoin was adopted as the global central bank in cyberspace?

The verifiable scarcity and transparency of bitcoin is unrivaled in its capacity to serve as the honest base layer for digital money. Better incentives will drive economies to create a better world for everyone. When money is scarce, physical property will become more abundantly available to everyone. If you suspect future bankers and politicians will be dishonest, then bitcoin is the most honest option for digital money.

To reiterate, real estate is not a reliable savings account. At any moment the price to buy real estate, hold real estate, or sell real estate could be raised beyond your ability to afford it. The lie of a working-class savings account has been sold by the Keynesian Kings to enrich an industry filled with money printing middlemen. They print new fiat money by selling mortgages to working people, and in turn, physically enslave job-locked workers to corporate masters. Outside of banks and government treasuries, no one is closer to the money printer than the real estate industry.

Who really benefits from home prices going up anyway? Your bank gets higher interest payments, your realtor and mortgage broker get higher commissions, your title company gets higher closing costs, and your government gets higher property taxes. What about you?

After you sell a home, you need shelter, so you buy your next home at a higher price. Only the housing industrial complex benefits from higher home prices.

The fear of your home value dropping in US dollars terms is anecdotal evidence, yet it illuminates the fiat bias we all must overcome. As we transition to a new economy where everything is repriced in bitcoin, lower home prices will not be feared but celebrated. When technology is allowed to reduce the costs to build new homes, property prices will fall against bitcoin. Lower home prices are better.

Once your property paradigm shifts, you will see real estate as a working-class casino where the housing industrial complex always wins.

I once heard bitcoin called "Love Your Neighbor Money." My instinctual reaction to this provocative statement was confusion. It wasn't until I understood bitcoin as a savings account that doesn't steal from people and is stripping away the monetary premium attached to shelter, precious metals, business ownership, and many other types of inefficient saving accounts that this label made sense to me.

In a Bitcoin economy where investor demand shifts away from physical property and towards digital scarcity, homes, gold, and stocks will return to their utility prices. As a former real estate investor, the idea of bitcoin's ability to lower home prices was a paradigm shift for me.

No technology could do more to financially revitalize the working class than to allow bitcoin to lower home prices for everyone. Housing is by far the greatest expense for the poor and middle class. One day, rich people will realize it is better to buy bitcoin instead of a second or third home — so someone else can afford to buy their first home. *That's* why bitcoin is "Love Your Neighbor Money."

When investors bid up the price of physical property, people who need that particular physical property for everyday life get hurt by higher prices. When investors bid up the price of bitcoin, no one gets hurt and everyone gets cheaper prices for the physical property they need for everyday life. Bitcoin allows investors to bid up property in cyberspace, and in turn, strip physical property of its monetary premium which will drive down the cost of physical property for everyone living in the physical world. Bitcoin is digital property for a better physical world.

STEALING YOUR SAVINGS

"You'll own nothing. And you'll be happy."[147] —World Economic Forum commercial.

In this final lesson on property, I will hypothetically attempt to steal from you. We are going to wargame the most popular types of property to test their ability to withstand a thief's attack. I want this exercise to inspire adversarial thinking in your mind. I want you to compare the theft and confiscation risk of bitcoin to other forms of property. We are going to wargame the theft of real estate, gold, stocks, bonds, fine artwork, collectibles, cryptocurrency, and bitcoin. My goal is to help you plan a proper defense of your property moving forward. Let's begin.

REAL ESTATE

Eminent domain. As the CEO of a property development company, I leverage my influential network to lobby local government officials, convincing them that my proposed economic development project would significantly benefit the community. I arrange for an official appraisal, undervaluing your property and leveraging legal loopholes in the eminent domain laws. Through strategic court filings and my connections, I expedite the acquisition process. Ultimately, the city seizes your property under eminent domain, then sells it to me for the economic development project. You lose your real estate and are forced to pay commissions and fees to buy a less valuable home.

Property tax foreclosure. As a lobbyist for a real estate investment firm, I leverage my political connections and instigate local governmental changes that result in a significant increase in property taxes in your neighborhood. Concurrently, I lobby for tightening property tax regulations, making the foreclosure process more swift and lenient. Unable to keep up with the higher tax payments, your property falls into a tax lien sale. Consequently, I acquire your property by purchasing this lien and eventually gain ownership through the foreclosure process.

Zoning devaluation. As a rich real estate investor and former city councilman, I leverage my extensive network to influence local policymakers to alter zoning laws favoring the establishment of a toxic landfill and an adult entertainment venue adjacent to your property. This, coupled with strategic rumors and news leaks about potential health and social issues, significantly devalues your property. As your property's worth drops below your outstanding mortgage balance, you are now underwater on your loan. Unable to refinance or sell for a profit, you are forced to default on your mortgage and face foreclosure, allowing me to get a cutback from the toxic landfill and adult entertainment businesses while legally acquiring your property for a discount.

War confiscation. As a general in the United States Army, I utilize my vast resources to ignite tensions between Republicans and Democrats, eventually escalating it into a full-blown conflict. Using my influence, I strategically place the conflict zone around your property, ensuring it will be a highly sought-after strategic point. Once the conflict ensues, your property is inevitably seized for military purposes. At the conflict's end, utilizing my connections with the victors, I am rewarded with your property as part of the post-war spoils.

Title theft. As a cybercriminal within a vast network of super-hackers, I employ a specialist in document forgery and manipulation to create seemingly authentic documents indicating a transfer of your property title to me. Simultaneously, using sophisticated hacking techniques, I infiltrate the county record's database to replace the original documents with these forged ones. By doing so, I seemingly become the legal owner of your property. Finally, I sell the property swiftly before any suspicion is raised, laundering the funds to protect my wealth. You are left with the liability and legal fees to prove you never transferred the title to your property.

Job loss. As a political activist and real estate investor, I create a situation leading to your dismissal from work — perhaps through a well-orchestrated campaign of misinformation, questioning your professional integrity or performance. As a result of losing your income, you struggle to keep up with the mortgage, taxes, insurance, and maintenance costs. This financial hardship eventually leads your bank to foreclose on your property. Subsequently, utilizing my wealth and connections, I purchase your foreclosed property at a reduced price from the bank.

Interest rate manipulation. As part of a central banking cartel, I influence monetary policy to aggressively increase interest rates. This sharp hike directly impacts your adjustable-rate mortgage, causing your monthly payments to skyrocket. Unable to afford the dramatically increased mortgage payments, you default on your loan, resulting in foreclosure. Then, using my extensive connections, I lower interest rates again and purchase your property through a foreclosure sale at a significantly reduced price.

HOA lien. As president of the Homeowners Association (HOA), I enforce strict, even potentially unjust, interpretations of the HOA rules, repeatedly penalizing you for minor or nonexistent violations and imposing hefty fines. As these fines go unpaid, the debt accumulates, and I exercise the HOA's power to place a lien on your property. Unable to settle the accumulated debt, the HOA then moves to foreclose on the lien. In the ensuing foreclosure sale, I leverage my resources to acquire your property at a reduced price.

Natural disaster. As the owner of a home insurance company, I cite certain exceptions or clauses in your policy, arguing that the specific nature of the natural disaster falls outside the coverages provided by your plan. Moreover, I assert that your failure to maintain the property adequately contributed to the total loss, using this as grounds to deny the claim. Faced with the enormous costs of rebuilding without insurance coverage, you are forced to sell the land. I then acquire your property at a considerably reduced price.

Crime spike. As the new city mayor, I make a controversial decision to significantly defund the local police department, which in turn leads to a marked increase in crime rates in your neighborhood. This surge in crime inevitably and drastically drives down the value of your property. As the property's worth drops below your outstanding mortgage balance, you fall underwater on your loan. Unable to refinance or sell for a profit, you default on your mortgage and face foreclosure. I buy the property at a reduced price.

Rent moratorium. As President of the United States responding to a global pandemic, I issue an executive order for a nationwide eviction moratorium to protect renters. With the moratorium in place, your tenants choose to withhold their rental payments, leaving you without your primary source of income for the property. Struggling to keep up with the mortgage payments, taxes, insurance, and maintenance costs without the rental income, you are unable to prevent the foreclosure on your rental property. Leveraging my network and resources, I then acquire your foreclosed property at a significantly reduced price.

Home builder supply. As a land developer with vast resources, I invest massively in the construction of low-income housing units in your area, dramatically increasing the supply. This sudden influx of low-income housing causes the value of your property to plummet due to the neighborhood's changing wealth demographics and market saturation. With the property value falling below your outstanding mortgage balance, your mortgage becomes underwater. Unable to recover from this financial setback, you default on your mortgage, leading to foreclosure, which allows me to acquire your property at a reduced price.

Forced occupancy. As an executive of Fannie Mae, I leverage our position as a major mortgage backer to introduce a controversial policy that mandates homeowners with extra space, like your family, to house homeless individuals. I use the legal precedent set by San Francisco's city regulations requiring businesses to house the homeless in their lobbies. I argue that since Fannie Mae owns a majority of your mortgage, we have the right to dictate usage of the property. If you refuse, we cite it as non-compliance and opt for foreclosure on the grounds of this violation. Consequently, I acquire your property through the foreclosure process.

GOLD

Counterfeit shares. As an expert counterfeiter at the trust that holds your shares of gold reserves, I exploit the near-identical density of tungsten to gold and create highly convincing gold-plated tungsten coins. When you request redemption of your shares, I provide these counterfeit coins, which on the surface appear to be legitimate gold coins. Considering the cost, difficulty, and specialized equipment required to detect gold-plated tungsten, you are unlikely to verify their authenticity unless you had a strong suspicion. Thus, you end up taking custody of essentially worthless coins, thinking you have converted your shares into physical gold.

Bank run. As a banker operating on a fractional reserve system, I issue gold certificates to borrowers, representing more gold than I actually hold in the bank, capitalizing on the assumption that not all depositors will demand their gold at once. With the high costs of securing physical gold and its indivisibility, most depositors are content to deal with the certificates instead. However, rumor spreads that my bank is insolvent. A bank run occurs and all depositors come to withdraw their gold simultaneously, but my bank does not have sufficient reserves to honor all the claims. In the bankruptcy, your gold is lost as my bank's assets are liquidated to pay off its debts.

Home invasion. As an armed robber with expert knowledge in locksmithing and safecracking, I discreetly break into your home and bypass your safe's security mechanisms. Once your safe is open, I quickly take your gold coins, which, due to their untraceable nature, offer an ideal loot. Gold can be quickly melted down, reformed, or sold without raising suspicion, making it impossible to trace it back to the original owner. With the gold in my possession and no identifying features, I disappear into anonymity.

Environmental activism. As President of the United States, in response to an environmental crisis, I promote a policy that prohibits private ownership of gold in order to discourage its toxic mining and associated mercury pollution. I show images of poor village children plagued by the death and destruction of toxic mining to inflame the ethical and environmental concerns of gold mining. I shift public sentiment against private gold ownership and effectively strip the purchasing power from your gold coins. Thus, under the guise of environmental activism, I essentially dispossess you of your gold.

Mining innovation. As CEO of Interstellar Mining, I am working on a way to profitably mine golden asteroids.[148] Unlike bitcoin, the supply of gold in the universe is unknown. Even with thousands of new bitcoin miners, I cannot increase the supply of bitcoin. With a thousand new rocket miners, I can increase the supply of gold. My goal is to commoditize gold so it can be used as a material in cutting-edge technology and hardware for everyone. If you hold gold as money, expect to be left holding salt when we accomplish the mission of our company.

National emergency. As the President of the United States, in response to a national emergency, I issue an executive order grounding all nonessential air traffic. This action, while potentially necessary for national security and public health reasons, effectively limits your ability to physically transport your gold bars for sale outside of your local area. Given the emergency situation, local demand for gold is insufficient or nonexistent as people prioritize essential supplies. This forces you to sell your gold at a significantly reduced price, if you can even find any buyers. Thus, by restricting your physical access to potential buyers, I indirectly devalue your gold and limit your ability to acquire necessary supplies during this national emergency — a covert form of theft.

STOCK PORTFOLIO

Political enemy. As a corrupt SEC official, I fabricate evidence to suggest that your portfolio is implicated in illegal trading activities, warranting an immediate investigation. With the centralized nature of your assets and the power bestowed upon the SEC, I swiftly freeze your account to prevent further transactions, effectively blocking your retirement plan. The compliant nature of your digital assets and trust in the financial system work in my favor, as your attempts to refute these charges are slow and arduous. Thus, I temporarily seize control of your financial future, exploiting the authority of my position and the complexities of financial law.

Patriotic tax. As President of the United States, I issue an executive order that seizes control of stock portfolios to fund global war efforts. Drawing from the precedent set by the 2013 Cyprus bank bail-in, I persuasively argue that this tax on the rich is a necessary measure for national survival, thereby gaining public support. Your brokerage account is forcibly taxed by 50% and the remaining 50% is converted into low-yield government war bonds. This move, while controversial, is justified under the guise of patriotism and societal responsibility. I effectively cancel your retirement plans and the State ultimately fails anyway.

Investment risk. As an incompetent risk manager, I make ill-timed and poorly researched investment decisions, selecting stocks that are vulnerable to interest rate hikes just as the Federal Reserve decides to raise rates. Given the inverse relationship between interest rates and stock prices, your portfolio's value plunges as the chosen stocks underperform in the unfavorable economic environment. This unfortunate combination of poor management and market circumstances drastically reduces the value of your stock portfolio, making it insufficient for your planned retirement. My poor timing and stock selections rob you of your timely retirement.

Competition complacency. As the CEO of a bloated S&P 500 company, I am comfortable sitting on my elite status. The gravy train of mindless contributions from tax-free pension and 401(k) retirement funds along with the protection I receive from government lobbying has incentivized my attitude of overconfidence. Unlike bitcoin's limited supply, there are an infinite number of startup companies targeting our market share. Last month, a new AI-driven competitor entered the market and is now offering a cheaper, faster, and easier product to our customers. I now see that rapid innovation is why the average lifespan of an S&P 500 company is expected to narrow to 12 years by 2027.[149] My company will be lucky to survive that long. Unless you sell your shares before I and my hedge fund friends do, then your retirement plans are wrecked.

COLLECTIBLES

Trusted expert. As a master counterfeit art dealer, I create an extremely convincing replica of a piece of fine art, taking care to mimic every detail and flaw to make the forgery almost indistinguishable from the original. I then sell you this counterfeit artwork, leveraging my reputation and the quality of the forgery to alleviate any doubts.

You only realize the deceit when you attempt to sell the artwork during your retirement and it's revealed as a fake by a more discerning expert, resulting in a significant loss.

Illegal purchase. As a master dealer in stolen art, I sell you a highly desirable and genuine piece of artwork, without disclosing its illicit origins. Leveraging my reputation and knowledge, I assuage any of your doubts and you purchase the artwork, considering it a valuable asset for your retirement. However, when you eventually try to sell the artwork during your retirement, it is identified as stolen, possibly through an international database of stolen art or a cautious expert. Consequently, you not only lose the expected revenue from the sale, but also the original purchase amount, effectively depleting your retirement funds.

Voided insurance. As a ruthless insurance agent, I use fine print within your insurance policy and the circumstances of your home theft to deny you reimbursement for your stolen antique vehicle. Pointing to a clause stipulating the necessity of specific security measures, I argue that your failure to install or maintain proper security constituted negligence on your part, thereby voiding your insurance policy. Consequently, despite your faithful insurance payments, you receive no compensation for your loss.

BONDS

Negative yield. As a presidentially appointed governor at the Federal Reserve, I convince my fellow six governors to stimulate inflation through policies such as quantitative easing and artificially low interest rates, effectively eroding the buying power of your bond portfolio. While your nominal returns might appear satisfactory, the rising inflation rate means that in real terms, your yield is increasingly insufficient. By maintaining artificially low interest rates, I create an illusion of positive return, when in reality, your buying power is subtly but steadily diminishing. So, under the guise of a booming bond market, your wealth is silently whisked away by the invisible hand of inflation.

Weapon of war. As a foreign Treasury official, I brandish your high-yield junk bonds as an economic weapon, declaring your home nation an adversary and hence, invalidating your investments. In this financial game of chess, your bonds become pawns sacrificed in a broader geopolitical dispute. Through these sanctions, your government feels the sting, but it is your bond portfolio that bears the brunt of the economic blow. Just like that, your retirement dreams are caught in the crossfire of international politics.

Political persecution. As a Treasury official, I am a puppet forced to dance to the tune of an executive order, seizing your bonds under the pretext of a national crisis. Our devious president, with a flair for the dramatic, spins a web of allegations, painting his political opponents — you included — as domestic terrorists. His cunning scheme rallies public support, giving him the mandate to issue the controversial bond confiscation order. And with the stroke of a pen, your bonds dissolve faster than a politician's promise after an election.

CRYPTOCURRENCY

Money printing. As lead alchemist of a crypto project, I conjure up a mountain of tokens for myself, a feat straight out of Medieval mythology. I spin golden tales about this protocol's potential, stirring a speculative cauldron of wash trading that boils over with an artificially bloated market cap. Then, in a grand display reminiscent of turning lead into gold, I sell all of my pre-mined tokens for bitcoin in one swift motion, leaving you clutching crypto tokens as valuable as fool's gold.

Hidden contract. As the founder of a crypto project, I assure you the token economics are transparently coded on the blockchain, while deceptively pulling the strings of clandestine, off-chain deals with vulture capitalists. The vultures receive a trove of pre-mined tokens at a steal of a price, their unlock schedules hidden in shadows away from any prying eyes on the blockchain. Like modern-day pied pipers, these vulture capitalists charm the masses on social media, all the while silently offloading their discount tokens at a premium to retail investors. Caught in this dance of deception, you are left clutching tokens as valuable as Monopoly money.

Phony ownership. As a digital artist, I create 10,000 digital generated monkey characters; each unique monkey is known as a non-fungible token (NFT). I engage in wash trading, where I set up a large network of digital wallets to buy and sell NFTs to myself. This creates the illusion that collectors are paying a lot of money for my artwork. In one of my marketing campaigns, a famous person I pay to build your trust convinces you that NFT ownership is a good investment because it is artwork securely stored on a blockchain. Caught up in the hype of skyrocketing NFT prices caused by my market manipulation, you set up a digital wallet and buy one of my digital monkeys for the price of a car. One month later, you walk down the street and see your digital monkey printed on a t-shirt. You sue the t-shirt manufacturer for intellectual property infringement. Your court system does not recognize NFT artwork ownership on a blockchain, so at the end of the day, you own a worthless line of code on a database which is disconnected from any real-world enforcement of intellectual property rights. Instead of paying me for a monkey NFT, you should have just taken a screenshot and printed your own t-shirt.

Regulation crackdown. As acting SEC chairman, I unleash a regulatory thunderbolt, accusing your cryptocurrency project of peddling unregistered securities. The aftershock jolts crypto exchanges into delisting your token faster than a scammer deletes social media accounts in a bear market. Caught in the seismic shift, your token's liquidity evaporates, leaving you clutching a database record as sellable as a waterlogged baseball card.

BITCOIN

For this final section of thievery, we will reverse outcomes and I will give you examples of common bitcoin theft attempts and how you can protect yourself. Whether you choose a Bitcoin signing device with single signature, multisignature, passphrases, or some futuristic biometric method to protect your Bitcoin private keys, the fundamental idea of bitcoin security will always remain the same. As Andreas Antonopoulos famously simplified in 2017, "Your keys, your bitcoin. Not your keys, not your bitcoin."[150] Let's begin your fight back against thievery.

Wrench attack. As a thug with a wrench, I rattle your nerves by breaking into your home and demanding your Bitcoin private key. With your cooperation, I snatch what seems to be your life savings, as easily as taking candy from a baby. However, little do I know that I have fallen for the oldest trick in the book; I stole your private key to a decoy Bitcoin address, a mere drip in the bucket of your total bitcoin savings. Meanwhile, the real treasure trove is hidden and safeguarded by a passphrase. The majority of your bitcoin remains in your possession.

Private key attack. As a state-employed whiz operating a supercomputer, I roll up my digital sleeves, attempting a brute-force attack on your Bitcoin private key. My battle, however, is against an unfathomable Goliath of mathematical odds: I must pick 12 out of 2,048 possible words and put them in the correct order to unlock your bitcoin. This amounts to a jaw-dropping 2^{128} possible word combinations, or 340,282,366,920,938,463,374,607,431,768,211,456 guesses[151] — a task that would take my supercomputer billions of years to solve. It is like finding a specific grain of sand in a universe filled with beaches, leaving me as flustered as a cat trying to catch a laser pointer.

Computer virus. As a shadowy crypto hacker, I create a devious digital bug to scurry into your computer, ready to pounce on your Bitcoin private key the moment it senses a connection. However, your air-gapped signing device, as reclusive as a hermit, never dares to touch the wild west of the internet. Instead, it communicates in cryptic whispers with the outside world through an interchangeable micro-SD card that pops in and out of your computer and signing device. Foiled by this offline guardian, my virus is as futile as trying to catch smoke with a butterfly net.

Online scam. As a slimy online scammer, my first trick is to dangle a tempting piece of YouTube bait in front of your eyes, promising a fantastical return of two bitcoin for every one you send to me — a digital Midas touch. When that illusion fails to ensnare you, I send a sly phishing email, masquerading as a convenient mobile wallet for your hardware signing device, hoping to snag your precious 12 words like a spider entrapping a fly. Yet, your digital wisdom shines through; you recognize this wolf in sheep's clothing, never revealing your seed words (except to a trusted backup device), leaving my devious plot as barren as a desert.

Stolen device. As a petty thief, I snatch your hardware signing device, grinning at my quick victory. But alas, after 12 futile attempts at guessing your pin, the device turns into a worthless brick. Meanwhile, you have already restored your bitcoin with your backup seed words and sent it to a new address. I am left with a dead device and a pit in my stomach as police sirens wail in the distance.

Exchange embezzlement. As the boss of a crypto exchange, I sell pretend bitcoin to my customers, tricking them with digital IOUs. But you are smart and withdraw bitcoin to your own signing device as soon as you buy it. Other people who store their bitcoin on my exchange find out too late that I have traded their bitcoin away. You kept your bitcoin safe in self-custody, so you avoid paying the cost of my embezzlement.

Yield risk. As the boss of a lending site, I tempt you to surrender your Bitcoin private key by promising interest payments on your bitcoin. But you are not fooled and keep your Bitcoin private key safe on your own signing device. Other people fall for my scheme and find out their bitcoin is gone when they try to withdraw it. My risky bets cost them their bitcoin, but yours was always safe because you never let me hold it.

—

What did you learn from this wargame exercise?

I hope this investigation into adversarial thinking helped you to grasp one important point: Trustless ownership is found only in a Bitcoin private key. You do not own physical property, especially real estate. What you actually own is a record in your state's database, guarded by your military under the condition that you follow all laws and pay all taxes. If you do not comply, your government will confiscate "your" real estate.

After examining the vulnerability of physical property to theft by governments, corporations, and thieves, you can now better understand the intention behind the World Economic Forum's declaration of "You'll own nothing. And you'll be happy." In a world without Bitcoin, their dystopian dream of global lordship over you is the most probable outcome. However, in a twist of events, Bitcoin was created in response to the 2008 great financial crisis to grant property rights to 8 billion people. You now have a way of owning the keys to your own property.

CONCLUSION

"Lost coins only make everyone else's coins worth slightly more. Think of it as a donation."[152] —Satoshi Nakamoto, June 21, 2010, BitcoinTalk.org.

Who is most likely to steal your bitcoin? You, ironically enough — through your own carelessness. Despite the greedy eyes of thieves, the most common way people lose bitcoin is through neglect and carelessness. With a casual shrug, many people neglect the best practices of seed phrase storage, treating it like a grocery list. One day, amid the chaos of life, signing devices, pins, and private keys go missing — irretrievable and lost forever.

Since 2009, it is estimated that more than 4 million bitcoin are lost forever due to private key mismanagement.[153] As Satoshi said, we should think of lost coins as an increase in scarcity and a donation to the purchasing power of others on the network. Going one step further, if you delay spending your bitcoin, you indirectly increase the purchasing power of someone who must spend their bitcoin today. In this way, the bitcoin incentive of future growth in purchasing power leads to delayed consumption that benefits the global poor who must spend their bitcoin to survive today. Beyond pristine property rights, Bitcoin is a blind global charity network with incentives designed to empower the poor.

While we are on the topic of incentives, I believe you will take self-custody and security of your Bitcoin private keys much more seriously only after you understand the full potential of bitcoin. Earlier in this chapter, we explored how other types of property are being awkwardly used today as inefficient money. Monetization of a new property, like bitcoin, has not happened since gold monetized more than 5,000 years ago.

As bitcoin absorbs the monetary premium from other types of property, bitcoin savers are positioned to be rewarded with life-changing gains in purchasing power while those who are last to let go of the fiat system are positioned to be hurt the most by its downfall. If you look at the market size of monetized properties being awkwardly used as stores of value, you can begin to forecast bitcoin's potential value.

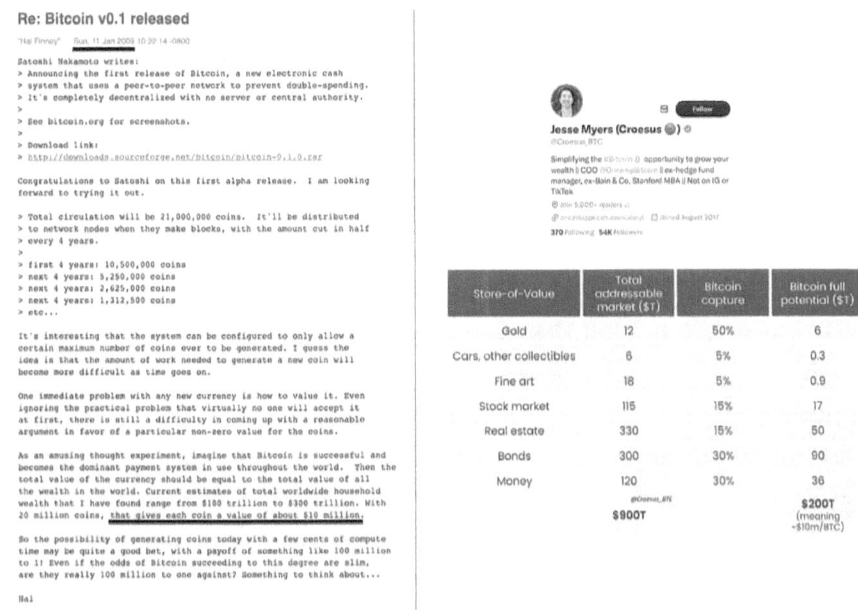

Re: Bitcoin v0.1 released

"Hal Finney"   Sun, 11 Jan 2009 10:22:14 -0800

```
Satoshi Nakamoto writes:
> Announcing the first release of Bitcoin, a new electronic cash
> system that uses a peer-to-peer network to prevent double-spending.
> It's completely decentralized with no server or central authority.
>
> See bitcoin.org for screenshots.
>
> Download link:
> http://downloads.sourceforge.net/bitcoin/bitcoin-0.1.0.rar

Congratulations to Satoshi on this first alpha release.  I am looking
forward to trying it out.

> Total circulation will be 21,000,000 coins.  It'll be distributed
> to network nodes when they make blocks, with the amount cut in half
> every 4 years.
>
> first 4 years: 10,500,000 coins
> next 4 years: 5,250,000 coins
> next 4 years: 2,625,000 coins
> next 4 years: 1,312,500 coins
> etc...

It's interesting that the system can be configured to only allow a
certain maximum number of coins ever to be generated. I guess the
idea is that the amount of work needed to generate a new coin will
become more difficult as time goes on.

One immediate problem with any new currency is how to value it. Even
ignoring the practical problem that virtually no one will accept it
at first, there is still a difficulty in coming up with a reasonable
argument in favor of a particular non-zero value for the coins.

As an amusing thought experiment, imagine that Bitcoin is successful and
becomes the dominant payment system in use throughout the world.  Then the
total value of the currency should be equal to the total value of all
the wealth in the world. Current estimates of total worldwide household
wealth that I have found range from $100 trillion to $300 trillion. With
20 million coins, that gives each coin a value of about $10 million.

So the possibility of generating coins today with a few cents of compute
time may be quite a good bet, with a payoff of something like 100 million
to 1! Even if the odds of Bitcoin succeeding to this degree are slim,
are they really 100 million to one against? Something to think about...

Hal
```

Jesse Myers (Croesus) @
@Croesus_BTC

Store-of-Value	Total addressable market ($T)	Bitcoin capture	Bitcoin full potential ($T)
Gold	12	50%	6
Cars, other collectibles	6	5%	0.3
Fine art	18	5%	0.9
Stock market	115	15%	17
Real estate	330	15%	50
Bonds	300	30%	90
Money	120	30%	36
	$900T		$200T (meaning ~$10m/BTC)

@Croesus_BTC

Source: Hal Finney, Jesse Myers.[154]

What if all goods and services are divided by a trustless, transparent, and fixed denominator of 21 million bitcoin, ∞/21M…?[155]

Under this scenario, Jurrien Timmer, Director of Global Macro at Fidelity Investments, believes that one bitcoin could be worth up to $1 billion by the year 2038.[156] Since human nature is unpredictable by nature, no one knows for sure when trust in the fiat system will be permanently broken; when it does happen, it seems likely that most of the global economy will quickly be re-priced in bitcoin.

American founding father, John Adams said, "Property must be secured, or liberty cannot exist."[157] If bitcoin is the most secure property on Earth, it can be used as an effective tool to fight the tyranny of time theft across the globe. The Bitcoin movement is working tirelessly to protect private property rights. If economic energy continues to be successfully password-protected, then bitcoin is better property for a better world.

A final word of warning, most of the cryptocurrency industry is designed to steal bitcoin from you. The discovery of digital scarcity can only happen once. I hope you will ignore the charlatan chatter of crypto casinos claiming to have discovered a better Bitcoin. The only way to create a better bitcoin is to have a creator who works for their coins, disappears, and leaves behind a leaderless global movement to fix money.

On Earth, only bitcoin gives you the ability to teleport economic energy across a thousand miles in your head or the potential to teleport economic energy across a thousand years from your deathbed. In summary, the two newly discovered properties of scarcity across time and capital portability across space make bitcoin better property for a better working class.

You have now learned why bad money makes life more expensive. Next, you'll discover why bad money can cost you your life. If the right to life, liberty, and the pursuit of happiness defines freedom, then it is worthwhile for us to consider the consequences of bad money on the first of these three self-evident truths, life. In our final chapter together, we will unpack the reasons why Bitcoin is better health for a better life.

5

HEALTH

"Truth is ever to be found in simplicity, and not in the multiplicity and confusion of things."[158] —Sir Isaac Newton, physicist, Warden and Master of the Royal Mint.

If your money is not what you thought it was, what else in your life is untrue?

Contrary to popular opinion, ignorance is not bliss. A life built upon lies is not a good life. The consequences of lies are not miraculously avoided by avoiding the truth. If you avoid the truth, your malleable mind will be manipulated to perpetuate propaganda.

What is propaganda? Propaganda is an orchestrated lie designed to dull your soul, divide your family, steal your money, and slowly give your life away to a malicious puppet master who wants to control your actions by manipulating your emotions.

On the brighter side, truth is a light, and light always overcomes the darkness of lies.

By learning about the nature of natural money, you have chosen to seek the light of truth. Your courage has disqualified you from being manipulated and controlled by the Keynesian Kings. Well done, truthseeker! Let's continue cutting the puppet strings of fiat money.

In Carlo Collodi's classic story of Pinocchio, this mischievous puppet avoids honest hard work which leads to dishonesty and numerous harsh consequences. Children are taught that being lazy and afraid of the truth makes it much easier to be fooled.

The scene that illustrates this lesson is when Pinocchio gets swindled by two thieves. A fox pretending to have a busted leg and a cat pretending to be deaf convince Pinocchio that if he buries his gold coins within the field of miracles, then his gold coins will sprout up into golden coin trees. This miraculous field is said to be located just on the outskirts of the city of Catch Fools. It turns out this city is populated by characters who sacrifice their future well-being for immediate satisfaction.

A little bird tries to warn Pinocchio that he is being lied to and the cat pretending to be deaf eats the bird.

How does Pinocchio fall for such a silly swindle? Pinocchio has the innocence of a child and a wooden brain, so he wasn't created with common sense. When the fairy who created Pinocchio asks what happened to his gold coins, Pinocchio lies, and his nose grows longer. Collodi hides a subtle lesson here: When we lie about stolen money, we grow farther away from the dream of being real boys and girls.

A wise boy will seek the truth and stand firmly on it when he finds it. The light of truth will sharpen your soul, reunite your family, save your money, and empower you to cut away the puppet strings of fiat propaganda — so you can live your life as a real boy.

What is life? Life is a mysterious force which hides itself from being seen directly by the human eye. Yet life's miraculous ability to transform billions of inanimate atoms into one living, breathing, conscious creature is plainly visible, but still remains beyond scientific explanation.

The closest scientists have come to measuring this invisible life force within us has been through developing our understanding of electricity. If you believe in a Creator, you may call the electricity that flows within your body, your soul. If you reject religion, you may call this electricity some type of electric charge passed on to you after your first ancestor was struck by a lucky lightning bolt.

Regardless of your philosophic point of view, there is a measurable amount of electricity within each of us. The First Law of Thermodynamics states that **energy cannot be created or destroyed**. It can only change form or be transferred from one object to another. According to this law of physics, when your time on Earth expires, the electricity within you will depart from your body and be transferred somewhere else.

Setting aside questions about life after death, let's use this concept of electricity as life-before-death to spark a conversation about the health benefits of bitcoin as natural money. What is natural money? Simply put, natural money mirrors nature.

Bitcoin is natural money because it respects the Law of Conservation of Energy. Like your time on Earth, bitcoin is limited. Like your life, Bitcoin requires electricity between lifeless atoms to power its network. Like a healthy economy, everyone must expend physical energy to bring new bitcoin into the money supply. Bitcoin respects nature by using limits and energy to create the most truthful record of money.

THE HEALING POWER OF HONEST MONEY

Why does truthful money matter to your health?

In economics, money is the nervous system of our economy and rising prices are the pain we feel when something is broken.

Imagine you fall from a tree and break your arm. Instead of paying a doctor to fix your painful broken arm, you decide to save money by taking painkillers to numb the pain. In the short term, you avoid paying for an expensive doctor bill, but what happens next?

You get addicted to painkillers, you begin to lie about everything to protect your addiction, and you take more and more pills to get the same numbing effect on your still broken arm. When you hit rock bottom of your addiction, you have two options:

1. You keep taking more and more pills until your liver stops absorbing the toxins. When your liver gives up, you die from an overdose.

2. You go to the doctor, pay to have him or her fix your broken arm, go to rehab, and stop taking the painkillers. You enjoy life and find a better tree to climb.

Let's unpack this Bitcoin parable:

- The human body is like the economy, with many parts working together as one organism to build a better world.
- The doctor is natural money, telling the truth about what is wrong in the economy and how to fix it.
- The broken arm is the pain of rising prices, where demand is high, but a supply chain is broken and needs to be fixed.
- The pain pills are like printing new fiat money to temporarily solve structural economic problems.
- The liver is the working class who absorbs the harmful side effects of fiat money printing.
- Option 1 is the choice to overdose by holding on to fiat money as the working class gradually rejects it as money.
- Option 2 is the choice to get better by admitting you have a money printing problem and adopting bitcoin as better money.

What are the costs of printing fiat money to numb economic pain?

In a healthy economy, more demand tells the market to get more innovative and create more supply. For example, if the price of bread goes up, bread producers should be monetarily motivated to increase the supply of bread and create more profit for themselves from the excess demand. Higher bread prices offer producers an attractive financial incentive to innovate and naturally increase the supply of bread, which would eventually lower the prices again.

Instead of allowing the free market to naturally lower prices, the fiat market forces producers to centralize power in order to bend the rules.

WHO PROFITS FROM THE DEATH OF AMERICA?

The inconvenient truth about fiat money is that food corporations are much better at bending the rules within a fiat economy than independent producers. Not only do their size, capital connections, and political influence give them better access to the fiat money printer, but they are also much better at swaying bureaucratic policies in their favor.

Common sense says the fiat food industry's unspoken political deal goes something like this:

Mega food corporations get more powerful by securing cheap loans that print new fiat money with which they buy up their smaller competitors. This unnatural money creation grows corporations into food giants. Most politicians and bureaucrats fear these corporate food giants and allow them to write their own regulations and subsidies. In exchange for governmental compliance, these corporate food giants build a revolving door between the regulators and highly paid corporate executives.

The fiat food giants lobby for lower food nutrition standards and get higher subsidies to maximize profits. Corrupt politicians get more powerful by printing more new money and relaxing nutrition standards which keeps food prices artificially stable in time for reelection.

What does the working class get from this fiat food industry deal? An obesity epidemic. Five decades of high inflation has left working people only able to afford highly processed fake foods coated with synthetic and highly addictive flavor dust.

Poor nutrition has resulted in skyrocketing rates of obesity, type 2 diabetes, and mental health disorders. The long-term nature of these chronic diseases offers plausible deniability to the people who manipulate your food and your money to hide the effects of fiat money inflation.

Not only is an unhealthy population more dependent on its government and therefore much easier to control, but an unhealthy population also generates more profits for the medical and pharmaceutical industries.

In 2021, medical costs related to obesity in the US surpassed $260 billion per year. An American obese person pays $3,097 more per year on healthcare costs such as inpatient treatment, outpatient treatment, and prescription drugs.[159] Who profits most from the $260 billion more dollars spent on obesity-related health problems each year? Time to follow the fiat money once again.

There is an unholy trinity of big government, big food, and big pharma that is profiting from the death of America. Look no further than the Pentagon's 2020 study on military readiness for evidence of the fiat food health epidemic. This study showed that 77% of young people do not qualify for military service due to being overweight, using drugs, or having mental or physical health problems.[160] For anecdotal evidence of how food quality has changed the health of young people, take a look at pre-1980 pictures of people and compare them to what you see today.

The crowded beach at Coney Island in the late 1950s.
Source: B.P., Stuff Nobody Cares About.[161]

In this 1977 file photo, theater goers wait in line to see "Star Wars."
Source: Paul Sorene, Flashbak.[162]

After 50 years of fiat money, we can clearly see the health effects: Bad money is bleeding the life out of America's poor and working classes.

The long-term nature of both debased money and debased nutrition gives politicians and bureaucrats the time and cover they need to blame others for the death of America. No one is being held accountable for the long-term side effects of fiat money devaluation.

To get the most out of this chapter, the key points you need to grasp are simple. First, dishonest money lies about everything, including what is healthy for you. Second, living farther away from the fiat money printer has health consequences.

Health is a controversial topic; everyone has an opinion about it. Rather than focusing on specific conclusions I have come to about how to navigate my own health under a fiat system, I want you to replace propaganda with common sense questions and draw your own conclusions.

Fiat money is a lie which has bestowed an unnatural amount of wealth upon a class of lying counterfeiters. If you want to live a healthier life, you must follow the money to discover the truth about your health. Even in a fiat system, money speaks louder than words. Following the fiat money trail will help you expose state-sponsored lies, isolate incentives, and identify who profits most from creating an unhealthy population.

As we discussed in Chapter 1, complexity in money breeds corruption everywhere. The same principle applies to the fiat healthcare system. From the image on the back of your dollar bill to the poster hanging up in your high school health education classroom, the fiat system is one big pyramid scheme meant to enrich the powerful money printers at the expense of poor people who work for the money they create for free.

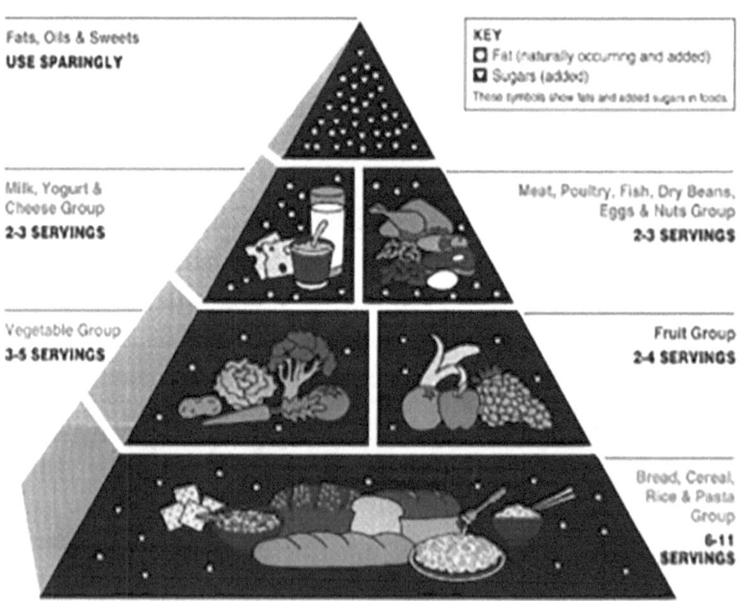

USDA Food Pyramid.[163]

Back of the US dollar bill.

SIMPLE IS BETTER

How can the unarmed light of truth conquer such seemingly powerful propaganda? According to Sir Isaac Newton, truth is ever to be found in simplicity. To find the truth, you should use your common sense to reject complexity and embrace simplicity.

Occam's razor is the time-tested method to reject complexity and better see the truth. This guiding principle of logic in philosophy suggests we should keep things as simple as possible to discover the truth. The success of the early Christian church is a prime example of this concept.

Within 400 years, a carpenter and twelve of his working-class Jewish students overthrew the state-sponsored Roman religion.[164] The new gospel message of Jesus was much simpler than paganism. Rather than man trying to appease thousands of gods, these new Christians believed a simpler message. Sin separates mankind from God and Jesus forgives sin to reconcile mankind with God.

This simple message of a Messiah and a forgiving Heavenly Father resonated with early believers, so much so that thousands were willing to endure persecution and even death to share this simple good news with others. Simplicity inspires long-term thinking, and among early Christian martyrs, even eternal thinking. To further illustrate the power of simplicity, Jesus was asked which of the 613 laws of Moses was most important.[165] No surprise, Jesus simplified the complexity of 613 laws into two commands:

"'You shall love Adonai your God with all your heart, and with all your soul, and with all your mind, and with all your strength.' The second is this, 'You shall love your neighbor <u>as yourself</u>.' There is no other commandment greater than these." —Mark 12:30-31 TLV.

Did you notice something here? Hidden within the second simple command from Jesus is an insinuation about your health. If you do not first love yourself, how can you love your neighbor <u>as yourself</u>? Taking care of yourself is a prerequisite to properly loving your neighbor. Whether you are a Christian or not, this simple truth about how you can love others better by loving yourself better likely connects as a simple truth.

Love never fails. Whether you lack exercise or lack nutritious food, let loving yourself and others be the reason behind improving your health.

Remember, success means something different for everyone. What you consider to be good health for you will be different from what I consider to be good health for me. Everyone is different, and perfect health does not exist. A healthy life is about progress, not perfection.

Driven by love and your newfound knowledge that fiat money is a liar, you are ready to begin seeking the truth about fiat food.

THE BIG FAT LIE

Before 1900, it was rare to die from heart disease or cancer in America. From 1900 to 2010, deaths per 100,000 people caused by heart disease rose by 40% and cancer deaths rose by 190%.[166] Pneumonia, influenza, tuberculosis, and gastrointestinal infections were the leading causes of death in 1900, but thanks to giant leaps in medical technology, Americans rarely die from these diseases today:

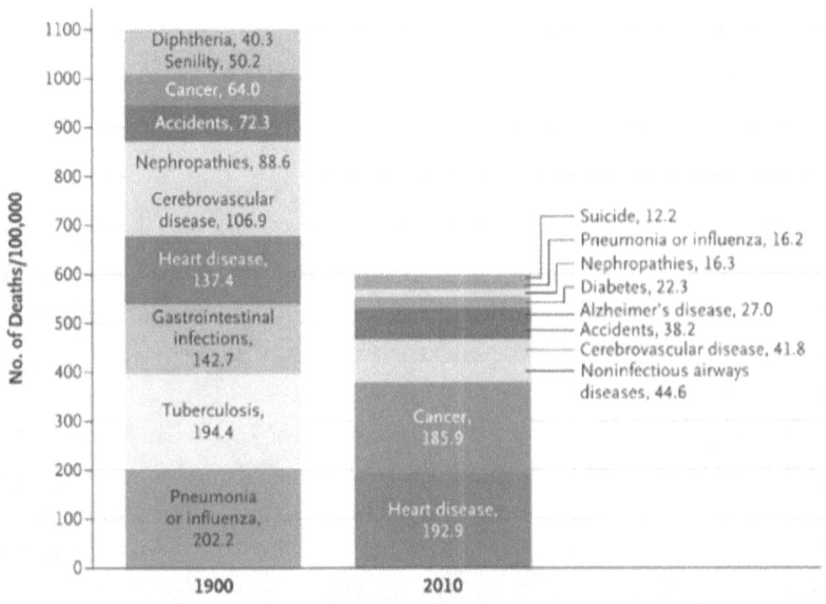

Source: Brian Fung, *The Atlantic.*

Over the last century, why did deaths from heart disease and cancer skyrocket while deaths from other deadly diseases dropped to almost zero?

During the 1900s, the biggest change to Americans' health was diet. Let's start by looking at the two biggest diet changes.

Diet Change #1: Vegetable oil

In June of 1911, Procter & Gamble introduced Crisco (crystalized cottonseed oil) into the American diet. They marketed this new edible oil as a more "pure" and economical alternative to traditional animal fats and butter.[167]

Throughout the industrial revolution, cottonseed oil was used as fuel for lamps and lubricant for machinery.[168]

In the early 1900s, William Procter and James Gamble were brothers-in-law who began experimenting with cottonseed oil to make soap. When the hydrogenated cottonseed oil hardened, the men noticed that it looked a lot like lard and asked, "Why don't we try to sell this as food?"

As to not spoil the appetites of people who only knew cottonseed oil as farming waste used in lamps and machinery, Procter & Gamble renamed this product vegetable oil. When you go out to eat, you see this same renaming tactic used by food marketers even today. For example, in modern times, "fried chicken" has almost universally become "crispy chicken" to avoid the unhealthy stereotype associated with fried food.

For thousands of years, our ancestors cooked with butter from cows, suet from sheep, and lard from pig fat. Now, thanks to a slick marketing campaign by Procter & Gamble, cheap industrial waste products were now seen by Americans as healthier fats. Common sense should have warned Americans that the cotton plant was not an edible vegetable, but sadly most Americans fell for the fake food propaganda.

Instead of human slaves picking the cotton seeds out of the lint, a new and subtle form of food slavery convinced the American working class to eat the cotton seeds. Encouraged by the success of this food propaganda campaign, in 1948, Procter & Gamble made a $1.7 million dollar contribution to the American Heart Association and coincidently, 13 years later their seed oil products were endorsed as heart healthy alternatives to saturated animal fats.[169]

By the 1950s, vegetable oil was marketed to sound much healthier than butter, tallow, or lard, and Americans ate it up.

Source: What I've Learned[168]

Before we move forward, it is difficult for me to imagine the biggest change to our human diet in over ten thousand years was unrelated to the creation of the Federal Reserve. Edible seed oils just so happened to occur two years before the Federal Reserve was founded and began manipulating American money. It is negligent to avoid following the fiat money with something as important as what we eat, so let's do it.

Who profited most from seed oils being introduced into the American diet? Food products made with seed oil are cheaper and have longer shelf lives. As the Federal Reserve increased the supply of dollars to pay for government overspending, politicians benefited from processed food manufacturers using cheap seed oils to lower food costs and hide food inflation from the American people.

Within 40 years of vegetable oils being introduced into the American diet, heart disease jumped from the number four to the number one cause of death in America. Instead of protecting Americans by recommending people return to the natural fats eaten by their ancestors, it appears politicians and processed food manufacturers chose to protect the money printer from the political ramifications of high food inflation.

By the 1950s, Americans were afraid: Healthy men were suddenly dropping dead from heart attacks. The Keynesian Kings saw this fear as an opportunity to control the American diet. All they needed was a good story to convince Americans that animal fats were killing people. One good story would cement their processed food pyramid scheme into a sustainable mechanism to hide food inflation.

Diet Change #2: Processed Food Pyramid

"On Saturday, September 24, 1955, President Dwight D. Eisenhower was playing golf at the Cherry Hills Country Club outside Denver. On the ninth hole, he started to complain about an upset stomach. He suspected that it was indigestion, since he had eaten a hamburger with slices of Bermuda onion for lunch. Nonetheless, he decided to call it a day, and he returned home. Shortly after midnight, he woke up with severe chest pain. He asked his wife, Mamie, for milk of magnesia, but she was concerned enough to call his personal physician, Dr. Howard Snyder."[170]

In the aftermath of President Dwight D. Eisenhower's heart attack, there were two views within the medical community of what was causing the heart disease epidemic. The battle was between sugar and cigarettes versus cholesterol and saturated fats. To explain the recent rise of heart disease, bureaucrats in Washington, D.C., chose to blame cholesterol and saturated fat and gave sugar and cigarettes a pass, but why?

It is time to follow the fiat money. In the 1950s, American men who appeared healthy were suddenly dropping dead of heart attacks, and the public wanted answers. Despite the fact that President Eisenhower was known to smoke up to three packs of cigarettes per day, the government needed to find a scapegoat that calmed American fears.

Eisenhower recovered from his heart attack and was reelected US President in 1956. One cardiologist working on President Eisenhower noticed physiologist Ancel Keys' work and placed Eisenhower on a strict low-fat diet. He ate less, exercised more, and followed his prescribed low-fat diet, yet he gained weight and his cholesterol rose to what some physicians might call dangerous levels.[171]

The low-fat diet ultimately failed President Eisenhower. He suffered from weight gain, stroke, type 2 diabetes, and multiple heart attacks before eventually passing away in 1969 due to intractable heart failure. Surprisingly, the American people failed to connect the death of President Eisenhower to his low-fat diet. The lack of public pushback opened the door for a full-fledged propaganda war against animal fats.

"In 1956, at a meeting of the American Heart Association in Chicago, Ancel Keys was already expounding his ideas about diet and heart disease."[172] From 1957 to 1970, like a clever prosecutor, Ancel Keys began building his case against animal fat consumption which culminated in publishing his results as the "Seven Countries Study." This study explored the relationship between saturated fat intake and cardiovascular disease.

Rejecting the scientific method, Keys launched his study as a way to **prove** his hypothesis that an ancient diet high in animal-based saturated fat was to blame for the relatively new phenomena of heart disease. Keys handpicked seven out of 22 studied countries that supported his hypothesis. Keys intentionally left out countries like Norway and Holland who ate a lot of saturated fat without a lot of heart disease, and countries like Chile that did not eat a lot of saturated fat and yet still had a lot of heart disease.[173]

Ancel Keys used his biased study to publish the "Diet Heart Hypothesis" which blamed animal fats for heart disease. Even Keys' advocates conceded his study was biased, yet it served as the launchpad for a fiat-funded crusade against the more costly animal fats remaining in the American diet.

In an effort to better influence government bureaucrats into supporting his flawed findings on heart disease, Ancel Keys joined the American Heart Association. One year later, with no new data, the American Heart Association adopted his unscientific recommendation that Americans should avoid eating animal products with high levels of saturated fat and cholesterol to reduce their risk of heart attack.

Uncle Sam officially got into the business of telling people what to eat when, in 1977, the McGovern Committee released its Dietary Goals for the United States. The conclusion of the committee was for people to increase carbohydrate consumption and reduce fat and meat consumption.

The American Heart Association endorsement paved the way for the US Department of Agriculture (USDA) to adopt Keys-inspired Dietary Guidelines in 1980 by recommending people, "avoid too much fat, saturated fat, and cholesterol."[174] The USDA effectively gambled American health by adopting Procter & Gamble's vegetable oil propaganda. This alignment of the American Heart Association and US Department of Agriculture gave birth to the low-fat, chemical-based food craze that followed.

In 1992, the USDA Food Pyramid was first released. The catchy food pyramid imagery placed fats, oils, and sweets at the top of the pyramid recommending that people eat such foods sparingly. It is ironically similar to a financial pyramid scheme, that the producers of the types of foods that were on the top of the pyramid became the richest in our fiat economy.

Not only the obvious fake food producers like Coca-Cola, but also food producers hidden within the recommended grain products. Grain products make up 40% of the recommended healthy diet, yet if you read the ingredients labels of breads and cereals you may be shocked by the irony. All of these processed grain foods are packed with sugar and seed oils, both of which the USDA recommends you eat sparingly.

Restaurants are the most dangerous place to eat vegetable oils. Repeatedly heated cooking oils (RCO) can generate compounds which have been reported as carcinogenic. According to the National Institute of Health (NIH), the large consumption of RCO has been associated with a number of malignancies, including lung, colorectal, breast, and prostate. Reheating oil in a fryer saves the restaurant money, but NIH warns the fumes and compounds have been shown to cause cancer by breaking down your cells and the DNA within your cells.[175]

Jeanne Freeland-Graves, division head of nutritional sciences at the University of Texas, explains, "You should never reheat oils. You're supposed to use them once and then throw them away. But in the food industry, they can't afford to do that. Good restaurants will change their oils and discard them, but that's expensive."[176]

What are the most harmful types of seed oils?

Studies show fried and processed foods with high levels of linoleic acid (LA) are most dangerous. Historic, pre-1930s levels of LA intake ranged between 1 to 2% of daily calories but averaged more than 7% of daily calories in 2011.[177] Processed foods like chips, crackers, salad dressings, and mayonnaise are loaded with the PUFA omega-6 fat, mostly from LA in seed oils. The oxidized end products of this acid are OXLAMS (oxidized LA metabolites) which damage the mitochondria and studies have shown lead to elevated rates of obesity, cancer, and heart disease.[178]

Cooking Oils	% Linoleic Acid (LA) Average Value (Range in Parentheses)
Safflower	70%
Grape seed	70%
Sunflower	68%
Corn	54%
Cottonseed	52%
Soybean	51%
Rice bran	33%
Peanut	32%
Canola	19%
Olive oil	10% (3% - 27%)
Avocado	10%
Lard	10%
Palm oil	10%
Tallow (CAFO)	3%
Ghee (CAFO)	2%
Coconut oil	2%
Tallow (Grass Fed)	1%
Ghee (Grass Fed)	1%

Source: lifesitenews.com.[179]

A University of California research study showed the compounds found in seed oils are likely linked to increased levels of obesity, diabetes, and even genetic changes in the brain.[180] Rather than adopting a stance on industrial seed oils, I hope you will instead agree on the importance of the question. If your dollar has been debased, in what ways has your diet been debased to hide food inflation?

For me, when it comes to food, my common sense says to trust nature more than scientists who attempt to transform industrial waste into cheap food. I recommend that you look up videos showing the manufacturing process for popular processed foods. As I watched videos of seed oils being acid washed, neutralized, bleached, and deodorized to hide the rancid smell and look of feces, I lost my appetite for fake food.

Simple logic has led me to conclude that our government and food corporations have propagandized us into fearing meat, cheese, butter, and eggs to hide food inflation.[181] Think about it. If we all stopped purchasing processed foods and economic demand switched to natural food, can you imagine the price hikes as supply chains are strained? There would be way too much fake money, chasing way too little real food.

For over a century, Americans have walked down the path of dollar-induced diet debasement. The results are in. Despite being the richest nation to ever exist, we are one of the sickest nations to ever exist. What if giant leaps in medicine were amplified by a return to better health from abundant nutrition? Instead of seed oils, pesticides, and chemicals, what if we supported better technology to empower local farmers?

As technology advances so rapidly, there is no reason to compromise our lives to keep the fiat system alive. If we allow technology to drive down the cost of food production for everyone, local farmers will be empowered by better technology to localize our food supply chains.

A local farmer could purchase a tractor to replace his pesticides with an AI-guided, pest-zapping laser. A fleet of humanoid robots could replace migrant farm labor, which is often exploited to keep food prices artificially low to hide inflation. As these new technologies get more affordable for local farmers on a bitcoin standard, the safety and quality of our food can become more affordable as well.

Bitcoin reverses the sticky price phenomena. If we build upon our exploration of economics in Chapter 2, instead of fiat money debasement incentivizing cuts in food quality to keep prices stable, bitcoin incentivizes an increase in food quality to keep prices stable. As food priced in bitcoin naturally falls in price over time, companies will compete to keep sticky prices by increasing the size and quality of their food products.

How do we peacefully transition away from a food industry built upon dishonest money?

Even if the truth turns out to be devastating to mainstream health narratives, moving forward we need courageous health researchers to expose the truth. A canary in the fiat health coal mine could be the 400,000 Amish people living in America. With a 4% obesity rate, the Amish population interacts with the modern world at local farmers markets, but do not partake in its processed foods, medicines, or electronics. These secluded people may be an unopened gift to measure health within our fiat system versus the more traditional ways of our ancestors.

"New Study Finds Zero Amish Children Diagnosed with Cancer, Diabetes or Autism."[182]

"Amish People Stay Healthy in Old Age. Here's Their Secret."[183]

"How The Amish Live Uninsured But Stay Healthy."[184]

As a reminder, I am a curious engineer who is learning to ask better questions; I am not a medical doctor, nutritionist, or epidemiologist.

Whether the above research is reliable or exaggerated is not my expertise. I do know my common sense tells me that studying the differences between the health of Amish people versus people living within the fiat system is a good idea. We need to measure fiat health versus non-fiat health to grade our healthcare system. If we cannot measure our health system we cannot improve it.

For thousands of years, our ancestors cooked with butter from cows, suet from sheep, and lard from pig fat. Common sense tells me that our human bodies know how to burn animal fats and may be confused by chemical foods. As the result of a weak and biased study by Ancel Keys, I have concluded that the free market of food has been manipulated to push fiat-funded propaganda that animal fats are killing people.

Whether it is cow flatulence causing climate change or animal fats causing heart attacks, it seems like the Keynesian Kings want to hide food inflation by encouraging working people to eat low-cost insects, seed-oil lubricant, and flavored chemicals instead of animal products.

I used to think the American obesity epidemic was a sign of prosperity. If you are poor and overweight, then you are not really poor by the world's standards. I still believe that poor Americans have a higher quality of life than a majority of the world's poor, however, after learning about inflation's influence on nutrition, I now believe it is more of a nuanced issue than I had previously concluded.

Are obese people eating more cheap junk food to feel full because processed foods lack any real nutrition? If so, modern obesity is more of a malnutrition problem than a gluttony problem. Malnutrition would explain why the working poor have been disproportionately impacted by the American obesity epidemic. Dishonest money has contaminated everything — including our food. It appears that cheap toxic food is being pushed onto poor people to protect those who run the fiat money printer from politically toxic food inflation.

Through the SNAP program in 2023, it is estimated the US government will spend $33 billion dollars on junk foods.[185]

Since the late 1970s, USDA data shows that for low-income individuals, average daily carbohydrate intake is up 26%, fat is up 11%, and protein is down 3%. The American obesity rate has soared from 15% up to 42% of adults during this same time period.

What change is the main culprit in the obesity epidemic?

The rise in carbohydrate consumption has coincided with a rise in consumption of junk food, loaded with soybean oil. According to Pew Research, since 1970 the consumption of cooking oils — mostly soybean oil — has increased by 250%, while the American consumption of beef has fallen by 33%.[186] Fiat food appears to be fattening Americans up like cattle before some type of socialistic slaughter.

Is diet debasement some type of Malthusian plot to reduce human population? Before we assign nefarious motives to the leaders within our fiat system, we should first consider looking at profit motives. Slaves are more profitable than graves. Fad diets, weight loss pills, cosmetic surgery, hospitals, insurance companies, and pharmaceutical corporations all profit more from obesity than from a healthy population.

With better money and better food, we can shift profits away from debt creators and toward local farmers who produce more nutritious foods.

If you count calories, you should also count ingredients. Simple money is better money and simple ingredients make for better food. Read your food ingredients label and if it looks like a science experiment, you have a crucial choice to make: Would you rather pay more for real food today or pay more for health problems later in life?

When you save in bitcoin, you naturally think more about the long-term consequences of your health decisions. Since bitcoin is designed to be worth more in the future, owning bitcoin motivates you to stay healthy so you can better enjoy your future savings.

Next, we follow the fiat money trail to figure out why and how truth is being censored to keep America's health problems unsolved.

CHRONIC CENSORSHIP

"Roger Ailes told me in 2014, and of course he was the founder and CEO of Fox News. I had participated in a documentary about the impacts of mercury in vaccines on neurodevelopment disorders in children. This sudden epidemic of neurodevelopmental disorders that had begun in 1989. And he [Roger Ailes] had a relative that he believed had been vaccine injured and he always would put me on his shows. I had this weird relationship with Roger Ailes because I had spent 3 months in a tent with him when I was 19 years old in Africa. And we had this friendship. He was a very clever and witty guy and he had not started Fox News. He had just left running the Nixon campaign communications and he had stepped down for The Merv Griffin Show. *But I had this lasting friendship with him. He was a very loyal friend, and he would always make the hosts of Fox News put me on to talk about environmental issues, so I was the only environmentalist for a decade that was going on Fox News.*

And I looked at him as sort of a Darth Vader for what he had done to American television and communications, but I still had this strange friendship with him, so he would always put me on, so I went to him to try to get on to talk about this documentary. He looked at it, his assistant Mike Lemente, who was running the station at the time looked at it and both of them loved it, but he said, "We can't let you on." And he told me at that time, if any of my hosts independently let you on to talk about this, I would fire them. I would have to fire them. And he said, "If I didn't fire them, I would get a call from Rupert Murdoch within 10 minutes." And he said to me, "75% of my evening news division advertising revenues are coming from pharmaceutical companies. Of the 22 ads on the typical evening news show, that typically 17 or 18 of those were pharmaceutical ads."[187] Jordan Peterson interview with Robert F. Kennedy Jr., June 11, 2023.

A common saying in Silicon Valley goes something like this: If you don't *pay* for the product, you are the product.

This silent deal between social media companies and their users has grown these tech giants to be worth hundreds of billions of dollars. When you sign up for a free social media account, your behavior patterns and personal information are sold to advertisers. There is no free lunch in economics. This is a well-known agreement between social media companies and their users, but a lesser known and more subversive arrangement exists within the legacy news media industry. Let's follow the fiat money.

Legacy news media makes part of its money by selling content to distributors. These distributors include cable, internet, and satellite companies. You pay a subscription fee to your distributor, but are you, the customer, paying the salary of your evening news anchor? What percentage of your subscription fee actually goes to the news channel creating what you watch?

According to 2020 market data from Kagan, the three major US cable news networks (Fox News, CNN, and MSNBC) generated $2.5 billion dollars in ad revenue. Advertising dollars represented about

44% of total cable news revenues.[188] Basic math implies that approximately half of cable news revenues come from distributor subscription fees and the other half comes from advertisers.

Legacy news media is in a 50/50 tug-of-war battle between pleasing their advertisers and their viewers.

The United States and New Zealand are the only two countries in the world where direct-to-consumer advertising of prescription drugs that include product claims is legal.[189] Most of us laugh as we watch cheesy drug commercials starring models acting out unrealistic life moments. We zone out as nauseating side effects of the drug are narrated by a voice in the background who suggests you should ask your doctor about it. Instead of questioning the effectiveness of these drug commercials to sell more pills, we should ask what other incentives are at play.

According to Kantar data (January 2020 – June 2021), Pharmaceutical ads were prime time news' biggest customers during the height of the COVID-19 pandemic. For ABC News their biggest advertiser was the pharmaceutical company Dupixent. MSNBC's biggest advertiser was the pharmaceutical company AbbVie, and four out of the top five CBS News advertisers were pharmaceutical companies.[190]

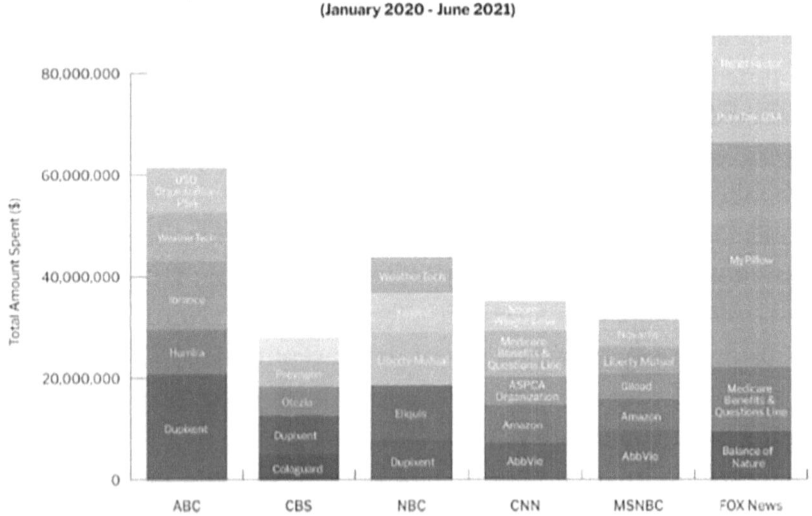

Data from Kantar Media/CMAG compiled by the UT Center for Media Engagement.[191]

What are the chances that pharmaceutical ads influence the news reporting on health issues?

It is naïve to think that legacy media is immune to monetary influence and corruption. Human nature tells us that executives will be persuaded by their paychecks to compromise truth at some point. During the COVID-19 pandemic, pharmaceutical companies were given billions of US tax dollars to develop MRNA vaccines.[192] The vaccines failed to stop transmission[193], and analysis by the Florida Surgeon General found that there was an 84% increase in the relative incidence of cardiac-related death among males 18-39 years old within 28 days following mRNA vaccination.[194]

Whether Donald Trump's Operation Warp Speed and Joe Biden's MRNA vaccine mandates cut corners on vaccine safety to enrich the pharmaceutical industry is beyond the scope of this book. The main point is fear led to medical censorship which resulted in bad decisions.

Rather than dig up more examples where health information was withheld from the public due to the influence of pharmaceutical advertisement dollars, like the story with Roger Ailes and Robert F. Kennedy Jr. above, I offer you a list of 12 better questions to ask yourself about the fiat health system:

1. What changed in the post-1971 American diet that led to a much unhealthier population today?
2. Do the medical and pharmaceutical industries profit more from chronic disease or good health in America?
3. How much influence does the pharmaceutical industry have over what health information is reported by the news media?
4. Why did the National Childhood Injury Act of 1986 exempt pharmaceutical companies from vaccine injury liabilities?[195]
5. Unlike other drugs, why are vaccines not required to pass long-term, placebo-controlled safety trials prior to licensing?[196]
6. Why have childhood vaccination schedules grown from 4 doses (1972) up to 60 doses (2022)?[197]
7. Why does the UK exclude chicken pox vaccines due to risk of deadly shingles outbreaks later in life, but the US does not?[198]

8. Why have autism rates grown from 1 in 2,000 children (1970) up to 1 in 36 children (2020)?[199]
9. Why did the FDA approve Merck's headache/arthritis drug Vioxx, which ended up killing up to 500,000 people?[200]
10. Is the FDA controlled by big pharma and if so, how often does the FDA mislead doctors within the American Medical Association?
11. Does fiat money creation through debt mining reward monopolies and corruption in medicine?
12. How can more transparency be achieved within the healthcare industry to expose bad actors?

To reiterate, the purpose of this book is to help you ask better questions about the side effects of fiat money, not to give you a prescription. Common sense suggests that to improve the healthcare system, the truth must be allowed to float to the top of our public discourse. Medical censorship must be rejected at all costs. Otherwise, complexity will be used by the Keynesian Kings to hide corruption.

With medical technology improving, we should see health and life expectancy improving as well. Poor diet, unsafe drugs, a desire for instant gratification, increased mental illness, and hopelessness for a better future are causing the American standard of living and life expectancy to plateau.[201] Perhaps a peer-to-peer money — bitcoin — can help usher in a more honest peer-to-peer healthcare system.

On a bitcoin standard, the healthcare industry's incentives will most likely be reconsidered and reimagined. Innovators will dream up a system where profits are maximized by a healthy population instead of a sick one. As long as human labor is not free, healthcare cannot be free. If the government makes healthcare a right, then healthcare providers must surrender their rights and be forced to work against their free will. The free market solution will most likely be a results-based system, where sickness and death are bad economics. If poor health is bad for the profits of healthcare companies, then economic incentives and health outcomes will change.

How can Bitcoin incentivize the healthcare industry to keep the world healthy?

A sick workforce means less productivity gains to drive down consumer prices in bitcoin terms. Higher prices will become bad for business. Robotics powered by AI may be allowed to drive down healthcare costs to near zero and free-up nonessential healthcare staff to work elsewhere. It may be as simple as prioritizing life over death, health over sickness, and work over debt creation to improve the quality of living for everyone. Let's close this chapter by exploring the most obvious yet counterintuitive way bitcoin can improve your health: cheap and abundant energy.

ENERGY ECONOMICS

"The Inflation Reduction Act of 2022 features tax credits for consumers and businesses that save money on energy bills, create jobs, make homes and buildings more energy efficient, utilize clean energy sources and lower greenhouse gas emissions that contribute to climate change and global warming."[202] —EnergyStar.gov.

Is energy reduction better for human life?

If you want the fiat money answer to this question, walk down the appliance aisle of your local home improvement store. If you want the Bitcoin answer, take a trek through the streets of an energy-impoverished country. Let's start at your local home improvement store.

As you walk down the aisle, look around and notice the political push for energy reduction all around you. The marketing stickers with promises of saving you money with Energy Star air conditioners, water heaters, refrigerators, washing machines, and dishwashers are impossible to miss. If the sticker promising to save you money on your electric bill is not enough to nudge you to reduce your energy consumption, then politicians sweeten the deal by offering you a federal tax credit of up to $3,200 per year.[203] When you buy the government's recommended products, you get to save money by reducing your energy usage and cashing-in on tax credits. Can you spot the ethical problem yet?

Not only does the EnergyStar.gov program empower the government to play favoritism by choosing which of its corporate friends get stickers and tax credits, but more importantly this type of government-sponsored marketing distorts buying decisions and creates an inefficient market.

When corporations adopt a political obsession like energy reduction that is backed by tax credits, innovation efforts get distracted. Instead of engineering new products for better performance, businesses ignore the free market and become obsessed with energy reduction to be competitive in the tax credit market. Eliminating wasted energy is good, but it is more efficient to eliminate the energy wasted by fiat money.

As a prime example of energy wasted by fiat money, President Joe Biden signed the $740 billion Inflation Reduction Act of 2022. Like all effective fiat propaganda, the name was meant to be misleading. The bill was not written to reduce inflation, which is primarily caused by government overspending. Instead, the bill included $369 billion in new spending to tackle climate change.[204] More specifically, the bill earmarked $265 billion in energy tax credits without $265 billion in government spending cuts.

The Keynesian Kings have abused the American people's fear of climate change and ignorance about fiat money to run multi-trillion-dollar federal budget deficits financed — by you guessed it — more inflation.[205]

What is most ironic here is that the Keynesian Kings who cause a majority of your inflation through excessive amounts of debt creation, they then turn around and try to sell you on the virtues of energy reduction. Big government and big business claim to be saving you money on higher electricity bills when, in reality, they are the ones that cause your electricity bills to go higher by adding more new money to the money supply.

From 1978 to 2023, data from the St. Louis Fed shows the average price of electricity in US cities has grown from $0.05 up to

$0.17 per kilowatt-hour.[206] Despite 45 years' worth of giant leaps in power generation technology, your electric bill continues to go up. During this same time period, the Keynesian Kings created 14.3 times more US dollars.[207] This is how they steal cheaper electricity bills from you.

Inflation has fueled higher energy prices and the EnergyStar.gov marketing program has manipulated the free market to compete on energy reduction. At what point does an inflation-ravaged, energy-impoverished working class become so poor that people prefer to save a few bucks on electric bills instead of buying better tools? When you imagine the innovation lost in this push for energy reduction, it is heartbreaking.

Thinking you can save the planet by reducing your energy consumption is like reducing the amount of sugar in your cake recipe each time you bake it; eventually you end up with a loaf of bread. You may still call it a cake, but it looks, tastes, and smells like bread. When you remove the energy from money, appliances, and people, you end up with a depressed and lifeless society.

The danger of continuing to walk down the aisle of energy reduction is that the Keynesian Kings may try to regulate the entire economy into a type of zero-emissions stone age for the working class. In this dystopian future, only the money-printing Keynesian Kings will be able to afford to pay for energy-efficient transportation, carbon taxes, and higher energy prices.

Bitcoin is hope that a full-fledged energy caste system can be averted. Now is the perfect time to recall the main takeaway from our previous chapter on economics. Bitcoin economics suggests scarce money will chase after abundant goods to drive down prices. On a fiat standard, energy reduction is simply a symptom of abundant money chasing after scarce energy, driving up prices in the process. On a bitcoin standard, power companies will chase scarce money by increasing the supply of energy and thus drive down your energy bills over time.

Within a bitcoin economy of falling energy prices, will energy efficiency still be important to you?

If you are an environmentalist concerned about climate change, you may still want to volunteer yourself as a tribute for these sadistic energy Hunger Games. I understand the image of smokestacks, smog, and a planet warming like a tropical greenhouse may come to your mind when you think of cheap abundant energy for everyone. Thankfully for the climate change crowd, the economic reality tells a different story.

Renewable energy is much cheaper to produce than fossil fuels.[208] If renewable energy is cheaper to produce than fossil fuels, then why are we still using fossil fuels? Many climate change activists blame the delay of green energy on the corporate corruption of big oil. Images of Dick Cheney, the Koch Brothers, and caricatures of greedy Republicans appear to be likely villains preventing our transition to renewable energy.

It appears there is some truth to the big oil conspiracy. After examining the Black Gold Standard in chapter 3, it is easy to spot the ethical dilemmas that arise from global dollars being pegged to fossil fuels. By now, you probably realize that voting for change is much less effective than changing financial incentives. From a purely economic perspective, renewable energy suffers from a transportation problem.

Let's talk about how Bitcoin can help to solve this renewable energy transportation problem. If you generate cheap renewable energy, you also need a cheap and reliable way to store and transport this energy across time and space. To transport renewable energy efficiently to its final point of consumption, you need an efficient battery mechanism. Since fiat money is divorced from energy and mined with debt creation, it is much cheaper to store and transport energy within a barrel of oil or a ton of coal than to build effective batteries.

In the pursuit of renewable energy batteries, rare earth mineral mining has skyrocketed and created its own environmental problems. The increasing demand for cobalt and lithium has empowered China, increased corruption in poor countries, exploited child labor, violated human rights, and led to landslides, groundwater contamination, and a larger $CO2$ footprint from the diesel-powered mining equipment.[209]

What if we rethink the definition of a battery? The purpose of a battery is to transfer energy across time and space. Bitcoin's proof-of-work protocol can be used as a type of battery for cheap renewable power production. This may sound far-fetched but follow me for a moment.

Did you know power plants must supply the exact amount of power demanded by the grid at any given time? When you look at your energy bill, this is why you see a range of rates depending on the time of day when you consumed the energy. Flexible rates add complexity to your electric bill and create inefficiencies for the power grid: By turning power plants on and off in reaction to fluctuating demand, energy is wasted.

Base load power plants cannot be turned off, so they generate a constant supply of cheap power to the grid. Without an efficient battery to match fluctuations in grid demand with fluctuations in the power generated by renewable energy, an inefficient work-around is used today. Base load power plants are supplemented by more expensive, "flexible" power plants, which are turned on and off to balance fluctuating renewable power supply with fluctuating grid demand. This inefficient process of balancing fluctuating energy supply and demand makes it impractical to implement non-subsidized renewable energy sources which, in turn, increases your energy bill.

What if bitcoin miners could buy electricity from base load power plants during periods of low grid demand?

Instead of wasting money on flexible power sitting idly and waiting for higher grid demand, reliable 24/7 energy consumption by bitcoin miners enables base power plants to be built that generate cheap energy supplies beyond peak levels of grid demand. By designing the power grid for excessive base load power, cheaper renewable energy could become the source continuously sold to customers. During low demand from the grid, base power plants will send their unneeded power to bitcoin miners as a way to stabilize/monetize low grid demand.

Without the heavy hand of government regulations or the costs of inflation and corporate corruption that come from subsidies, the free market economics of bitcoin mining can solve the unaffordable renewable energy problem. Bitcoin miners can be turned on to mine bitcoin when grid demand is low, and turned off when grid demand is high. Building excess renewable power supply into base power plants is much cheaper and more efficient for power companies than turning flexible power plants on and off.

One of the most common criticisms of Bitcoin is the energy consumed by its proof-of-work protocol to mine new bitcoin. You have probably heard that Bitcoin uses more energy than large countries. Without digging into the economics of energy production, this sounds like a wasteful practice compared to fiat money. But upon deeper consideration, bitcoin miners are playing the important role of 24/7 energy buyers.

Bitcoin miners do not drive up your energy costs. It would be economic suicide for bitcoin miners to hook up to your power grid and pay retail rates for electricity. Instead, profit motives drive bitcoin miners to search for, and develop, cheap stranded energy sources to remain profitable.

Everywhere you see movement in nature is unrealized energy. From the simple movement of ocean tides to the complex chemical reactions caused by the burning of fossil fuels, energy is the force behind the movement of atoms within our universe.

Most renewable energy on Earth is stranded from the grid, but bitcoin mining changes energy economics. Renewable energy pioneers seeking to capture new energy sources can monetize their off-grid research from day one by selling their power to the Bitcoin network. With fiat money, power produced by renewable research projects is stranded from the grid marketplace and wasted. Bitcoin mining does not "waste" energy — it recycles wasted energy. If Bitcoin is a reliable 24/7 buyer of energy, it becomes a battery to supply abundant energy to everyone.

The primary cost of bitcoin miners is energy. This means the future of bitcoin mining likely belongs to power companies who can produce the cheapest and most reliable energy to mine for new bitcoin. When new money from bitcoin mining flows to power companies instead of banks, so will the brain power and financial incentives for civilization-changing innovation. Power companies will invest in cutting-edge research and development projects to capture the cheapest renewable energy to mine more bitcoin, and in turn, benefit everyone with lower energy prices.

By discussing the energy economics of bitcoin mining, you may feel that we have gone off-track and are distracted from our health discussion. Nothing could be further from the truth. No factor impacts health more than energy economics. It is now time to take a trek through the streets of an energy-impoverished country to discover why bitcoin is better energy access for a better life.

ENERGY POVERTY

My palms are sweating as I board the plane for a 17-hour flight. This is my first international mission trip, and the first time leaving my wife behind. Our team includes two US Marines, a mortgage broker, a youth pastor, an entrepreneur, and me — the indispensable database engineer.

In the months leading up to this expedition, I trained by breathing through straws and running on a fully inclined treadmill. I expect the physical strain of trekking up high-altitude mountains with low levels of oxygen to be the most challenging part of the trip. I am wrong.

Boarding the plane to start this journey is by far much more difficult than any physical challenge that lies ahead. When the plane's wheels go up, there is no turning back: I am traveling to the other side of the world.

I step off the plane in Kathmandu. I am excited to get to work delivering Nepali Bibles to remote mountain villages.

Unexpectedly, the local airline canceled our final flight from Kathmandu to Pokhara. Instead of waiting until tomorrow for the final 90-minute flight, we decided to hire a local to drive us eight hours across the Himalayan mountains — in a minivan. The narrow two-lane mountain roads to Pokhara are carved into thousand-foot sheer cliffs. We share these narrow roads with large transport trucks. There are many times when I look down and see that our minivan wheels are inches aways from sliding off of the mountain.

The winding roads stir a Nepali pastor to vomit on the back of my mortgage broker friend; we stop the van at a local village to clean up.

This little village in Nepal is where my sympathy for energy poverty really begins. For the first time in my life, I walked through a village with no electricity. Every indoor room is hot and muggy. The restrooms are nothing more than outhouses with holes in the ground that smelled of steaming pungent sewage. The hopeless look on the faces of these downtrodden people still bothers me to this day.

After my friend changes his t-shirt and cleans up our van, we jump back on the narrow mountain road toward Pokhara. We drive past beautiful waterfalls dropping ice-cold, gray water over rugged granite cliff sides. We drive past the greenest rice fields cut into the mountainside with snow-capped mountains as their neighbors. The farther we get outside the capital city, the better is the scenery — and the worse is the poverty.

Apartment buildings connected by tangled electrical lines in the capital city gradually transition into single-room huts without any electricity. This is what it is like to live in a country with a per-capita income of $799 per year.[210] After this experience, I will never be the same.

As my team and I trek 50 miles over five days, we visit a handful of remote villages tucked away in the Himalayan Mountains. Most of the local villagers are very warm and welcoming to us. One peculiar thing I notice is that many people do not have insulated shelter, running water, shoes, or electricity in their homes — but almost everyone owns a smartphone.

It is perplexing that people choose to buy a smartphone and charge it with a community generator instead of first setting up electricity, running water, and owning a decent pair of shoes. Why is communication valued above basic utilities? After years of contemplating this odd observation, the answer finally hit me. The choice is not about valuing communication over basic utilities, it is about energy access.

Every Nepali village on my trek was surrounded by abundant supplies of hydroelectric energy. Endless supplies of hydropower from rivers and waterfalls could electrify this country. Why hasn't it happened? Energy economics. The low-income demographics of these remote villages left no profit incentive for a power company to come in and build the infrastructure necessary to transfer hydropower from the rivers and waterfalls to the people. Energy economics drives energy poverty. Thankfully, bitcoin mining changes energy economics.

BITCOIN MINING SAVES LIVES

"About 3 billion people in the world do not have access to modern energy sources for cooking and heating their homes. They are suffering from indoor air pollution as a consequence and millions die every year."[211]

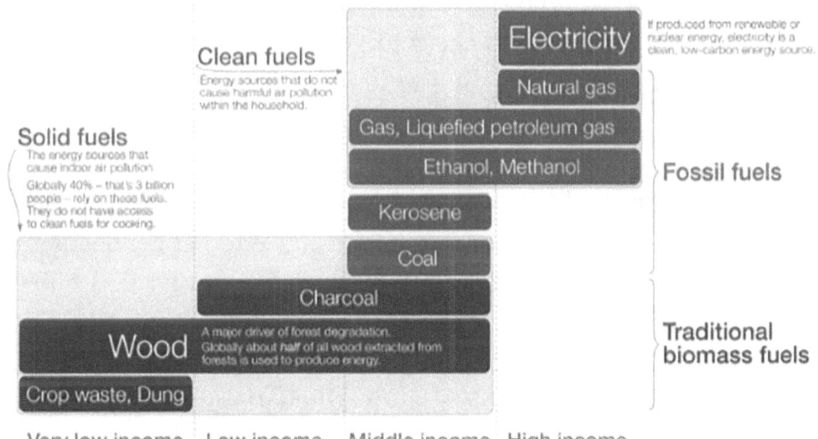

Source: Max Roser, "Energy Poverty and Indoor Air Pollution"[211]

Without reliable energy access, millions of people die. The World Health Organization estimates that 40% of the world cannot afford energy for heating and cooking within their homes, and as a result, 3.8 million people die every year from indoor air pollution. Pneumonia, COPD, lung cancer, heat stroke, and elevated rates of stillborn births are caused by burning crop waste, dung, wood, and charcoal in the home.

The danger of heating and cooking with toxic pollutants inside of the home means the consequences of death and disease from energy poverty primarily impact women and little children at much higher rates than adult men.

Before access to electricity, the life expectancy of Americans in 1900 was 48 years old. After electricity, it grew to 79 years old in 2014.[212] Nepal has a life expectancy of 69 years old.[213] Sub-Saharan Africa is the most energy-impoverished region in the world, with a life expectancy of about 59 years old.[214] When people lack access to affordable energy, decades worth of life is lost.

People with access to affordable energy live longer and healthier lives. Affordable energy helps children survive childhood, live longer, eat better, drink cleaner water, and learn new skills after sunset. Expanding access to reliable and affordable energy saves lives.

Imagine you wake up in the middle of the night to the sound of your child crying and struggling to breathe. You rush to the hospital and arrive to find the doctors cannot operate their life-saving equipment because of a power outage. This is the reality for billions of people without access to reliable electricity. More than 100,000 health facilities in Africa lack access to reliable electricity and internet connectivity.[215]

Energy poverty is the main reason why 74 out of 1,000 Sub-Saharan African kids die before their fifth birthday.[216] Compare this to about 5 out of 1,000 American kids and you begin to see the true costs of unreliable and unaffordable energy. Life without energy is poverty and death.

Living things consume energy; dead things do not consume energy. Dead things reduce their energy consumption to zero and ultimately give energy back to other living things. Energy reduction is life reduction. Energy is life, so we should use Bitcoin to produce more energy, not less.

Energy has been drained from the dollar. To create new dollars, you need only to mine the energy necessary to be approved as worthy of being issued a loan from a fractional reserve bank. Debt creation does nothing to alleviate energy poverty.

Unlike debt-mined fiat money, bitcoin is energy-mined. If fiat mining rewards new debt creation, then bitcoin mining will reward new energy creation. Power companies will be financially rewarded with new money supply as they grow the supply of energy. Basic economics suggests that supply and demand determine prices. If bitcoin mining increases the supply of energy, prices will go down and your health will be better.

CONCLUSION

Bitcoin is not about profit; it is about people.

Sir Isaac Newton wrote, "*Truth is ever to be found in simplicity, and not in the multiplicity and confusion of things.*"[217] For the last century, the Keynesian Kings have exploited the complexities of fiat money to create widespread chaos and confusion about money, economics, politics, property, and health. The Keynesian Kings have waged a war on currency, and truth has been its greatest casualty.

Dishonest money contaminates everything, including your body.

Even if clever fiat food marketers continue to advertise their seed oil as vegetable oil, fried chicken as crispy chicken, and obesity in a box as heart healthy, I hope you will now see past the fiat propaganda and use your common sense to ask better questions.

Follow the fiat money to discover who may benefit from turning you into a trash bin for corporate waste spewed out by the industrial food complex. Do not surrender your common sense to corporations and bureaucrats who want to keep their hand in the cookie jar of fake money.

You were not born to become a return-on-investment for consuming the Keynesian Kings' fake food products. Regardless of how much bitcoin you own, without good health, you are broke. Natural food may seem expensive today, but what's more expensive are the medical bills and pharmaceutical pills that will most assuredly catch up with you later in life. Let Bitcoin inspire hope in a better future and lead you to live better.

If fiat money fuels deception in every aspect of your life, how do you price truthful money against deceitful money?

Instead of wondering whether now is a good time to buy bitcoin, I hope you now see bitcoin as a voluntary choice to not participate in the lies fueled by fiat money. To save your money in bitcoin is to peacefully protest the corruption of the Keynesian Kings who are happy to profit from your pain and sickness. Bitcoin is an investment in a future filled with more affordable nutrition, healthcare, and energy access for everyone.

Nothing did more to propel economic prosperity forward in America than access to cheap and abundant fossil fuels. Relentless innovation in the extraction of fossil fuels through horizontal drilling, fracturing, and offshore exploration offset money printing to make post-1971 inflation tolerable. We are nearing the cost floor of diminishing returns for fossil fuel innovation, and bitcoin mining can help us take a giant leap forward. The up-front costs of renewable energy innovation can be offset by bitcoin mining and unlock an era of abundant energy access for everyone.

In the beginning, I said I hope this book helps you ask better questions so you can make an educated decision on whether Bitcoin is better for you. I hope you have made time to rethink what the future of money, economics, politics, property, and health look like after Bitcoin.

Do you trust public code more than central bankers?	Bitcoin is better money.
Do you trust inventing new technology more than printing new money to make life more affordable?	Bitcoin is better economics.

Do you trust politicians with limited budgets more than politicians with unlimited budgets?	Bitcoin is better politics.
Do you trust mathematics more than political property protection?	Bitcoin is better property.
Do you trust nature more than bureaucrats and corporations?	Bitcoin is better health.

Bitcoin is a bridge to better health and a better life. Instead of prescribing more complex fiat money printing to alleviate the woes of the working class, nature has prescribed a simple solution. Bitcoin is natural money that works for the working class. Bitcoin is better.

Get Involved

"I believe that unarmed truth and unconditional love will have the final word in reality."[218] *—Martin Luther King, Jr., Nobel Prize acceptance speech (1964).*

Unlike government money, the Bitcoin code cannot arm itself and force you to work for it. You choose bitcoin when you are ready for an unarmed, truthful money. You choose bitcoin when you are ready for unconditional money that is open to your friends and foes alike.

Working without a bitcoin savings account is like trying to run a race with an open wound. With each stride, the blood rolls down your leg and you are drained of the energy you need to run the race to the best of your abilities. This is what it is like to work without bitcoin. If you choose to leave your wound open, you are underperforming in the race of life and inviting economic parasites to feast on your energy leak.

Within the fiat money system, there will always be economic parasites who aspire to reap money without sowing energy. They feast upon the ignorance, apathy, and stubbornness of workers who won't stop long enough to ask better questions, seek the truth, and fix their energy leaks.

Satoshi Nakamoto is like a beaver who built a better dam based on the nature of natural money. This dam is leak-proof money that harnesses working-class energy to protect and propel the value of honest work forward into the information age. After adopting bitcoin, you become like a beaver. When you hear the sound of rushing water in your own life, you instinctively seek truth and take action to plug all of your energy leaks.

When I realized the potential for better money to make so many other things better, I couldn't stop talking about it. I wanted to tell everyone I loved that fiat money was stealing energy from them — and bitcoin was a better option.

Watching the 2022 Super Bowl ads, with commercials starring celebrities that pushed bitcoin **and** cryptocurrency, motivated me to write this book. Like other forms of evil, stealing energy through money printing takes on many different forms. I think it is just as important to expose dishonest cryptocurrencies as it is to expose dishonest fiat money. Instead of more money flowing into bitcoin, billions of dollars flowed from the working class into the pockets of crypto founders, marketing firms, and celebrities who endorsed get-poor-quick schemes for personal gain.

The lingering consequence of the 2022 Crypto Crash is that now most of the working class incorrectly associates bitcoin with multi-billion-dollar crypto scams like Luna, FTX, BlockFi, and Celsius. The next wave of bitcoin adoption must be different.

Bitcoin is a social network. Like all social networks, Bitcoin gets better when more people use it. I am founding a non-profit to help grow sustainable bitcoin adoption within the working class. As Henry Ford wrote: The people must be helped to think naturally about money.

In chapter 1 of Genesis, God did not make the world perfect: He made it good to leave room for you and me to make it better. If you would like to help me introduce bitcoin as natural money that works for the working class, please get involved by visiting: www.bitcoinisbetter.org.

References

Adams, John. *The Works of John Adams Volume 6: Defence of the Constitution IV Discourses on Davila*. Altenmünster, Germany: Jazzybee Verlag (2015).

Adams, John. "To Jonathan Jackson," Amsterdam, Oct. 2, 1780. Available via National Archives, Founders online: https://founders.archives.gov/documents/Adams/06-10-02-0113

Agovino, Theresa. "Merck Knew Vioxx Dangers in 2000," *CBS News*, Jun. 22, 2005: https://www.cbsnews.com/news/merck-knew-vioxx-dangers-in-2000/

American Deposit Management. "History of Quantitative Easing in the U.S." Accessed Aug. 14, 2023 via: https://americandeposits.com/history-quantitative-easing-united-states/

Ammous, Saifedean. *The Bitcoin Standard: The Decentralized Alternative to Central Banking*. Hoboken, NJ: John Wiley & Sons (2018).

Ammous, Saifedean. *The Fiat Standard: The Debt Slavery Alternative to Human Civilization*. Saif House (2021).

Analyze & Optimize. "Why is Vegetable Oil in Everything? | The History and Corruption Behind Processed Oils," *YouTube*, Sept. 1, 2019: https://www.youtube.com/watch?v=OGLwGOvvWeg

Antonopoulos, Andreas. "Not Your Keys, Not Your Bitcoin," *YouTube*, Sept. 17, 2018: https://www.youtube.com/watch?v=gB4wrX2iICA&ab_channel=TinyCryptoBlog

Architecture News. "How Many Houses Are in the World?" *Architecture and Design*, Nov. 11, 2021: https://www.architectureanddesign.com.au/features/list/how-many-houses-are-in-the-world

Auken, Ida. "Welcome to 2030. I Own Nothing, Have No Privacy, and Life Has Never Been Better," *World Economic Forum*, Nov. 11, 2016. Archived via:

https://web.archive.org/web/20161125135500/https://www.weforum.org/agenda/2016/11/shopping-i-can-t-really-remember-what-that-is

B.P. "Coney Island Beach Crowds From July 4's Of The Past," *Stuff Nobody Cares About*, Jul. 4, 2018: https://stuffnobodycaresabout.com/2018/07/04/coney-island-crowds/

BBC. "Slave Beads, West Coast of Africa, 1780s," A History of the World, available via: https://www.bbc.co.uk/ahistoryoftheworld/objects/SFN5MChbTPe9jKIKCDnD-g

Beigel, Ofir. "Bitcoin Historical Price & Events," *99Bitcoins.com*, Jan. 15, 2023: https://99bitcoins.com/bitcoin/historical-price/

Bell, J.L. "'No Taxation Without Representation' (Part 1)," *Journal of the American Revolution*, May 21, 2013: https://allthingsliberty.com/2013/05/no-taxation-without-representation-part-1/

Benz, Ernst Wilhelm, Lindberg, Carter H., Chadwick, Henry. "The Alliance Between Church and Empire," *Encyclopedia Britannica*, Jul. 22, 2023: https://www.britannica.com/topic/Christianity/The-alliance-between-church-and-empire

Bernholz, Peter. *Monetary Regimes and Inflation: History, Economic and Political Relationships.* Cheltenham, UK: Edward Elgar (2003).

Bernstein, Jules. "America's Most Widely Consumed Cooking Oil Causes Genetic Changes in the Brain," University of California, Riverside, Jan. 23, 2022: https://www.universityofcalifornia.edu/news/americas-most-widely-consumed-cooking-oil-causes-genetic-changes-brain

Bertaut, Carol, von Beschwitz, Bastian, and Curcuru, Stephanie. "The International Role of the US Dollar," *FEDS Notes*, Oct. 6, 2021: https://www.federalreserve.gov/econres/notes/feds-notes/the-international-role-of-the-u-s-dollar-20211006.html

Bhatt, Gita. "Keynes, the IMF, and the Future," *IMF Blog* May 30, 2019: https://www.imf.org/en/Blogs/Articles/2019/05/30/keynes-the-imf-and-the-future

Bible, King James Edition: Matthew Available via Bible Gateway: https://www.biblegateway.com/passage/?search=Matthew%2012:24-26&version=KJ21

Bible, King James Edition: Matthew. Available via Bible Gateway: https://www.biblegateway.com/passage/?search=Matthew%207:14-16&version=KJ21

Bitcoin Mining Council, "Global Bitcoin Mining Data Review Q4 2022," Jan. 2023: https://bitcoinminingcouncil.com/wp-content/uploads/2023/01/BMC-Q4-2022-Presentation.pdf

Black, William K. *The Best Way to Rob a Bank Is to Own One: How Corporate Executives and Politicians Looted the S&L Industry.* Austin, TX: University of Texas Press (2005).

REFERENCES

Blackburn, Henry. "On the Trail of Heart Attacks in Seven Countries," University of Minnesota, Driven to Discover. Available online via: https://sph.umn.edu/site/docs/epi/SPH%20Seven%20Countries%20Study.pdf

Blinkley, Collin. "Test Scores Show How COVID Set Kids Back Across the US," *PBS NewsHour*, Oct. 24, 2022: https://www.pbs.org/newshour/education/test-scores-show-how-covid-set-kids-back-across-the-u-s

Board of Governors of the Federal Reserve System. "Credit and Liquidity Programs and the Balance Sheet." Accessed Jul. 23, 2023: https://www.federalreserve.gov/monetarypolicy/bst_crisisresponse.htm

Board of Governors of the Federal Reserve System. "Policy Tools: Reserve Requirements." Mar. 15, 2020: https://www.federalreserve.gov/monetarypolicy/reservereq.htm

Boatwright, Mary T., Gargola, Daniel J., and Talberg, Richard J.A. *A Brief History of the Romans*. New York: Oxford University Press (2006).

Booth, Jeff. *The Price of Tomorrow: Why Deflation is the Key to an Abundant Future*. Stanley Press (2020).

Booth, Jeff. "Abundance in Money = Scarcity Everywhere Else," *Twitter* Jul. 2, 2022: https://twitter.com/JeffBooth/status/1543291963117473792

Bordo, Michael D. "Gold Standard," in *EconLib: Concise Encyclopedia of Economics* (2007). Available online via: https://www.econlib.org/library/Enc/GoldStandard.html

Brown, Elizabeth. "Feudalism," *Encyclopedia Britannica*, Jun. 30, 2023: https://www.britannica.com/money/topic/feudalism

Bush, George. "State of the Union with Candy Crowley," *CNN*, Dec. 16, 2008. Available via YouTube: https://www.youtube.com/watch?v=NaIxqJu_m2M

C.J. Trent-Gurbuz. "What Are Seed Oils and Are They Bad for You? A Comprehensive Guide," *US News*, Mar. 13, 2023: https://health.usnews.com/wellness/food/articles/what-are-seed-oils-and-are-they-bad-for-you

Caplan, David and Dwyer, Devin. "Elizabeth Warren: I'm 'Troubled' by Obama's $400,000 Speaking Fee for Healthcare Conference," *ABC News*, Apr. 28, 2017: https://abcnews.go.com/Politics/elizabeth-warren-troubled-obamas-400000-speaking-fee-healthcare/story?id=47071428

CDC. "Data & Statistics on Autism Spectrum Disorder." Centers for Disease Control and Prevention, Apr. 4, 2023: https://www.cdc.gov/ncbddd/autism/data.html

CDC. "History of the 1918 Flu Pandemic." Centers for Disease Control and Prevention, Mar. 21, 2018: https://www.cdc.gov/flu/pandemic-resources/1918-commemoration/1918-pandemic-history.htm

Chan, Terry and Dimitrijevic, Alexandra. "Global Debt Leverage: Is a Great Reset Coming?" S&P Global, Jan. 13, 2023. Available via: https://www.

spglobal.com/en/research-insights/featured/special-editorial/look-forward/
global-debt-leverage-is-a-great-reset-coming

Chandler, Marc. "The Dollar Rules the Financial Universe. China Can't Change That," *Barrons*, Mar. 31, 2023: https://www.barrons.com/articles/dollar-china-petro-yuan-saudi-b0b6e48f

Chesterton, G.K. *The Everlasting Man*. London: Hodder & Stoughton (1925). Available online via Project Gutenberg: https://gutenberg.org/cache/epub/65688/pg65688-images.html

Children's Health Defense. "Vaccine Makers Do Not Use Placebos to Test the Safety of Their Vaccines for Kids." Available online via: https://childrenshealthdefense.org/vaccine-secrets/video-chapters/vaccine-makers-do-not-use-placebos-to-test-the-safety-of-their-vaccines-for-kids/

Clayton, Stephen. "Money." Everyday Economics, by the Federal Reserve Bank of Dallas, Nov., 2015. Available online via: https://www.dallasfed.org/~/media/documents/educate/everyday/money.pdf

Congressional Research Service. "The International Monetary Fund," *In Focus*, Mar. 7, 2022: https://sgp.fas.org/crs/misc/IF10676.pdf

Congressional Research Service. "The U.S. Dollar as the World's Dominant Reserve Currency," *In Focus*, Sept. 15, 2022: https://crsreports.congress.gov/product/pdf/if/if11707

Crisco.com. "Our Heritage: 1911-Present." Available via: https://crisco.com/our-heritage/

Croucher, Shane. "Fact Check: Were There 600,000 Southern US Border 'Got-Aways' in 2022?" *Newsweek*, Dec. 29, 2022: https://www.newsweek.com/southern-us-border-migrants-gotaways-2022-1770201

Davis, Carole and Saltos, Etta. "Dietary Recommendations and How They Have Changed Over Time," in Elizabeth Frazão (ed.), *America's Eating Habits: Changes & Consequences*: 33-50. US Department of Agriculture: Washington D.C (1999). Available online via: https://www.ers.usda.gov/webdocs/publications/42215/5831_aib750b_1_.pdf?v=41055

Dematos, Daniel. "The Decline and Fall of Roman Coinage," The Tontine Coffee-House: A History of Finance, Aug. 12, 2019: https://tontinecoffeehouse.com/2019/08/12/the-decline-and-fall-of-roman-coinage/

Desilver, Drew. "Most U.S. Bank Failures Have Come in a Few Big Waves," Pew Research Center, Apr. 11, 2023: https://www.pewresearch.org/short-reads/2023/04/11/most-u-s-bank-failures-have-come-in-a-few-big-waves/

DeSilver, Drew. "What's On Your Table? How America's Diet has Changed Over the Decades," *Pew Research Center*, Dec. 13, 2016: https://www.pewresearch.org/short-reads/2016/12/13/whats-on-your-table-how-americas-diet-has-changed-over-the-decades/

Doheny, Kathleen and Chang, Louise. "Autism Cases on the Rise; Reason for Increase a Mystery." *WebMD*, Mar. 28, 2008: https://www.webmd.com/brain/autism/features/autism-rise

Donnelly, Sue. "Hammering out a New World — the Fabian Window at LSE," *LSE Blogs*, Sept. 13, 2017: https://blogs.lse.ac.uk/lsehistory/2017/09/13/hammering-out-a-new-world-the-fabian-window-at-lse/

Dowell, William. "Foreign Exchange: Saddam Turns His Back on Greenbacks," *Time*, Nov. 13, 2000: https://content.time.com/time/subscriber/article/0,33009,998512,00.html

Dr. Cate. "Cholesterol: What the American Heart Association is Hiding from You (Part 2)," Drcate.com, Jan. 7, 2021: https://drcate.com/cholesterol-what-the-american-heart-association-is-hiding-from-you-part-2/

Edison, Thomas. "In an Unusual Talk with Allan L. Benson," March 1929, *Hearst's International Combined with Cosmopolitan*, 83. Quoted in Garson O'Toole, "As a Cure for Worrying, Work Is Better Than Whisky," *QuoteInvestigator* Nov. 26, 2016: https://quoteinvestigator.com/2016/11/26/work-whisky/

Edwards, Chris. "The Hidden Cost of Our Huge Problem With Obesity," *Fox News*, Jul. 3, 2023: https://www.foxnews.com/opinion/hidden-cost-huge-problem-obesity

Elflein, John. "Total Number of US COVID-19 Cases and Deaths April 26, 2023," *Statista*, May 2, 2023: https://www.statista.com/statistics/1101932/coronavirus-covid19-cases-and-deaths-number-us-americans/

Energy Star. "Tax Credit Legislation," Dec. 30, 2022: https://www.energystar.gov/about/federal_tax_credits/tax_credit_legislation

Everett, Burgess, Otterbein, Holly, and Wu, Nicholas. "'The Weirdest Legislation That Anybody Has Ever Been Asked to Vote on,'" *Politico*, Jun. 1, 2023: https://www.politico.com/news/2023/06/01/progressive-anger-debt-deal-00099541

Evers-Hillstrom, Karl. "Most Expensive Ever: 2020 Election Cost $14.4 Billion" *OpenSecrets*, Feb. 11, 2021: https://www.opensecrets.org/news/2021/02/2020-cycle-cost-14p4-billion-doubling-16/

Exposito, Alyssa. "Nearly 4 Million Bitcoin Will Probably Never Be Recovered — Here's Why," *MarketRealist*, Dec. 21, 2021: https://marketrealist.com/p/how-much-bitcoin-is-lost/

FDIC. "Statistics At A Glance," Sept. 30, 2022. Available online via: https://www.fdic.gov/analysis/quarterly-banking-profile/statistics-at-a-glance/2022sep/fdic.pdf

Federal Reserve Bank of Atlanta. "All About Project Hamilton," *Talk About Payments* Webinar, Jun. 9, 2022. Archived online via: https://archive.li/HVkOQ.

Federal Reserve Economic Data (FRED) "Median Family Income in the United States" (MEFAINUSA646N). Available via: https://fred.stlouisfed.org/series/MEFAINUSA646N

Federal Reserve Economic Data (FRED). "30-Year Fixed Rate Mortgage Average in the United States" (MORTGAGE30US). Available online via: https://fred.stlouisfed.org/series/MORTGAGE30US

Federal Reserve Economic Data (FRED). "Assets: Total Assets: Total Assets (Less Eliminations from Consolidation): Wednesday Level" (WALCL). Available via: https://fred.stlouisfed.org/series/WALCL

Federal Reserve Economic Data (FRED). "Average Price: Electricity per Kilowatt-Hour in U.S. City Average" (APU000072610). Available via: https://fred.stlouisfed.org/series/APU000072610

Federal Reserve Economic Data (FRED). "Federal Debt Held by Federal Reserve Banks" (FDHBFRBN). Available via: https://fred.stlouisfed.org/series/FDHBFRBN

Federal Reserve Economic Data (FRED). "Federal Debt Held by Foreign and International Investors" (FDHBFIN). Available via: https://fred.stlouisfed.org/series/FDHBFIN

Federal Reserve Economic Data (FRED). "Federal Funds Effective Rate" (FEDFUNDS). Available via: https://fred.stlouisfed.org/series/fedfunds

Federal Reserve Economic Data (FRED). "M2" (WM2NS). Available via: https://fred.stlouisfed.org/series/WM2NS

Federal Reserve Economic Data (FRED). "Median Sales Price of Houses Sold for the United States" (MSPUS). Available via: https://fred.stlouisfed.org/series/MSPUS

Federal Reserve History. "Emergency Banking Act of 1933," Nov. 22, 2013: https://www.federalreservehistory.org/essays/emergency-banking-act-of-1933

FedPrimeRate. "Dow Jones Industrial Average History (DJIA / Dow 30)." Available online via: https://www.fedprimerate.com/dow-jones-industrial-average-history-djia.htm

FiatMarketCap. "Top Fiat Currencies by Market Capitalization." Accessed Jul. 24, 2023: https://fiatmarketcap.com/

Finney, Hal. "Re: [bitcoin-list] Bitcoin v0.1 released." Satoshi Nakamoto Institute, Jan. 11, 2009: https://satoshi.nakamotoinstitute.org/emails/bitcoin-list/threads/4/

Flink, James J. "The Automobile and the Transformation of American Life," *Journal of American History* 62, 2 (Sept., 1975): 512-529.

Florida Health. "State Surgeon General Dr. Joseph A. Ladapo Issues New mRNA COVID-19 Vaccine Guidance." Bulletin, Oct. 7, 2022: https://content.govdelivery.com/accounts/FLDOH/bulletins/3312697

Ford, Henry. *My Life and Work*, in collaboration with Samuel Crowther. New York: Doubleday, Page & Company (1922).

Foundation Devices. "Make 12 Words the Standard," Foundationdevices.org, June 2023: https://foundationdevices.com/2023/06/make-12-words-the-standard/

Fraser, Matthew. *In Truth: A History of Lies From Ancient Rome to Modern America.* Lanham, MD: Prometheus Books (2020).

Freeman, Dean. "Rare Earth Mining: The Dark Underside of Sustainability," *3DinCities*, Apr. 20, 2021: https://www.3dincites.com/2021/04/rare-earth-mining-the-dark-underside-of-sustainability/

Friedman, Milton. *Monetary Mischief: Episodes in Monetary History.* New York: Harcourt Brace & Company (1992).

Frontier Center. "2020 International Property Rights Index," *FCPP.org*, Nov. 24, 2020: https://fcpp.org/2020/11/24/2020-international-property-rights-index/

Fung, Brian. "Chart: What Killed Us, Then and Now," *The Atlantic*, Jun. 22, 2012: https://www.theatlantic.com/health/archive/2012/06/chart-what-killed-us-then-and-now/258872/

Ganesan, Kumar, Sukalingam, Kumeshini, and Xu, Baojun. "Impact of Consumption of Repeatedly Heated Cooking Oils on the Incidence of Various Cancers — A Critical Review," *Critical Reviews in Food Science and Nutrition* 59, 3 (2019): 488-505.

Garcia, Ariana. "NASA to Voyage to 'Golden Asteroid' Worth $10,000 Quadrillion This Fall," *Chron*, Jun. 11, 2023: https://www.chron.com/news/space/article/nasa-golden-asteroid-18144519.php

Giesecke, Oliver. "Changes in the Intended Federal Funds Rate, 1971-1992," Board of Governors of the Federal Reserve System, Washington, D.C., Aug. 29, 2019: https://www.federalreserve.gov/foia/files/20190829-changes-intended-federal-funds-rate.pdf

Gjelten, Tom. "Defense Officials Anticipate Drop in Military Spending," *NPR*, Jul. 6, 2010: https://www.npr.org/templates/story/story.php?storyId=128320487

Gladstein, Alex. *Hidden Oppression: How the IMF and World Bank Sell Exploitation as Development.* Nashville, TN: Bitcoin Magazine Books (2023).

Glavinskas, Vanessa. "The Inflation Reduction Act is a Victory for the Climate. Here's What Comes Next," *Vital Signs*, Environmental Defense Fund, Sept. 6 2022: https://vitalsigns.edf.org/story/inflation-reduction-act-victory-climate-heres-what-comes-next

GotQuestions. "What are the 613 commandments in the Old Testament Law?" GotQuestions.org, available via: https://www.gotquestions.org/613-commandments.html

Greenspan, Alan. "The US Can Pay Any Debt it Has Because it Can print Money to Pay it!" *NBC News* Meet the Press, Aug. 7, 2011: https://www.youtube.com/watch?v=-_N0Cwg5iN4

Gregersen, Erik. "History of Technology Timeline," *Encyclopedia Britannica*, Jan. 15, 2019: https://www.britannica.com/story/history-of-technology-timeline

Harris, Alexander. "US Self-Storage Industry Statistics," SpareFoot StorageBeat, Jan. 27, 2023: https://www.sparefoot.com/self-storage/news/1432-self-storage-industry-statistics/

Hartill, Robin. "What Rate of Return to Expect From Your 401(k)" *The Motley Fool*, May 9, 2023: https://www.fool.com/retirement/plans/401k/returns/

Higgs, Robert. "How U.S. Economic Warfare Provoked Japan's Attack on Pearl Harbor," *Independent Institute*. May 1, 2006: https://www.independent.org/news/article.asp?id=1930

History.Com. "Mesopotamia: The World's Earliest Civilization," *History.com*, Nov. 30, 2017: https://www.history.com/topics/ancient-middle-east/mesopotamia

History.Com. "This Day in History: United States Freezes Japanese Assets," *History.com*, Nov. 16, 2009: https://www.history.com/this-day-in-history/united-states-freezes-japanese-assets

Holzer, Henry Mark. "How Americans Lost Their Right To Own Gold And Became Criminals in the Process," *Brooklyn Law Review* 39, 3 (Winter 1973): 517–550.

https://www.worldatlas.com/articles/countries-by-percentage-of-world-population.html

Huxen, Keith. "The 1944 Bretton Woods Conference," The National WWI Museum, Nov. 29, 2019: https://www.nationalww2museum.org/war/articles/1944-bretton-woods-conference

Ironman. "The Price History of Campbell's Tomato Soup," Political Calculations, Jan. 19, 2023: https://politicalcalculations.blogspot.com/2023/01/the-price-history-of-campbells-tomato.html

Jefferson, Thomas. "To Colonel Carrington," Paris May 27, 1788. In *The Works of Thomas Jefferson*, volume 2: 403-405. Edited by H.A. Washington. New York: Townsend Mac Coun (1884).

Johns Hopkins University (JHU) Coronavirus Resource Center. "Mortality Analyses," Mar. 16, 2023: https://coronavirus.jhu.edu/data/mortality

Jordà, Òscar, Knoll, Katharina, Kuvshinov, Dmitry, Schularick, Moritz, and Taylor, Alan M. "The Rate of Return on Everything, 1870-2015," *Quarterly Journal of Economics* 134, 3 (Aug. 2019): 1225-1298.

Kennedy, Robert F. Interview on "The Faulkner Focus." *Fox News*, Jun. 2, 2023. Available online via: https://www.youtube.com/watch?v=AArdEpHQSI0&ab_channel=FoxNews

Kennedy, Robert F. Jr. "Obamacare Changed the Democratic Party," DailyWire+, Jordan B. Peterson Clips, via *YouTube*, Jun. 11, 2023: https://www.youtube.com/watch?v=bnUVU6pB-J8

Ketcham, Ralph L. *The Political Thought of Benjamin Franklin*. Indianapolis/Cambridge: Hackett Publishing Company (1953[2003]).

Keynes, John Maynard. *The Economic Consequences of the Peace*. Cham, Switzerland: Palgrave macmillan (2019).

Khorram-Manesh, Amir, Burkle, Frederick M., Goniewicz, Krzysztof, and Robinson, Yohan. "Estimating the Number of Civilian Casualties in Modern Armed Conflicts–A Systematic Review" *Frontiers in Public Health* 9 (Oct. 2021). Available online via: https://www.ncbi.nlm.nih.gov/pmc/articles/PMC8581199/

Kim, Yujin, Murray, Caroline, Jomini Stroud, Natalie, and Muddiman, Ashley. "Advertiser Spending on Primetime News Throughout the Coronavirus Pandemic," The University of Texas at Austin, Center for Media Engagement (Mar. 2022). Available online via: https://mediaengagement.org/wp-content/uploads/2022/03/Advertiser-Spending-on-Primetime-News-Throughout-the-Coronavirus-Pandemic-1.pdf

King, Martin Luther Jr. "Acceptance Speech," NobelPrize.org, Dec. 10, 1964: https://www.nobelprize.org/prizes/peace/1964/king/acceptance-speech/

Kluger, Jeffrey. "Amish People Stay Healthy in Old Age. Here's Their Secret," *Time*, Feb. 15, 2018: https://time.com/5159857/amish-people-stay-healthy-in-old-age-heres-their-secret/

Krebsbach, Jared and Lambrecht, Eric. "What Role Did Inflation Play in the Collapse of the Roman Empire?" *DailyHistory.org*, Nov. 22, 2018: https://dailyhistory.org/What_Role_Did_Inflation_Play_in_the_Collapse_of_the_Roman_Empire

Laurence, Emily and Acosta, Rafael Sepulveda. "Obesity Statistics," *Forbes Health*, Jun. 13, 2023: https://www.forbes.com/health/body/obesity-statistics/

Lee, Yoojung. "How Many Millionaires in the World?" *Bloomberg*, Sept. 22, 2022: https://www.bloomberg.com/news/articles/2022-09-20/world-will-get-more-millionaires-after-2022-s-wealth-destruction

Lewis, Michelle. "Two-Thirds of New Renewables Were Cheaper Than Coal in 2021 – IRENA," *Electrek*, Jul. 7, 2022: https://electrek.co/2022/07/14/renewables-cheaper-than-coal/

REFERENCES

Lewis, Nathan. "The Federal Reserve in the 1920s 2: Interest Rates," *New World Economics*, Nov. 25, 2012: https://newworldeconomics.com/the-federal-reserve-in-the-1920s-2-interest-rates/

Lincoln, Abraham. "Reply to a Committee from the Workingmen's Association of New York," Mar. 21, 1864, in *Complete Works* X. Available online via Abraham Lincoln Association Serials at the University of Michigan: https://quod.lib.umich.edu/a/alajournals/0599998.0005.008/49?page=root;size=100;view=text

Little House. "How's That For Inflation?" Little House in the Valley, Jul. 21, 2011: https://www.littlehouseinthevalley.com/hows-that-for-inflation/

Longley, Robert. "The Currency Act of 1764," *ThoughtCo*, Oct. 2, 2020: https://www.thoughtco.com/currency-act-of-1764-104858

Lund, Robert W. "Horse-Drawn Carriage Industry in America: The Final Days," *Business History Review* 42, 3 (Autumn 1968): 369–382.

Macias, Amanda and Franck Thomas, "Biden Administration Expands Sanctions Against Russia, Cutting off U.S. Transactions with Central Bank," *CNBC*, Mar 1, 2022: https://www.cnbc.com/2022/02/28/biden-administration-expands-russia-sanctions-cuts-off-us-transactions-with-central-bank.html

MacroTrends. "Nepal Life Expectancy 1950-2023." Available online via: https://www.macrotrends.net/countries/npl/nepal/life-expectancy

Manuel, Frank E. *The Religion of Isaac Newton*. Clarendon Press: Oxford (1974).

Mark, Joshua J. "Ancient Egyptian Taxes & the Cattle Count," World History Encyclopedia, Feb. 7, 2017: https://www.worldhistory.org/article/1012/ancient-egyptian-taxes--the-cattle-count/

Masterson, Victoria. "What Does 'Global Debt' Mean and How High is it Now?" *World Economic Forum*, May 16, 2022: https://www.weforum.org/agenda/2022/05/what-is-global-debt-why-high/

Meek, Andy. "As Fox News Turns 25, Here's How Its Business Stacks Up Against Rivals CNN And MSNBC Andy Meek," *Forbes*, Oct. 12, 2021: https://www.forbes.com/sites/andymeek/2021/10/12/as-fox-news-turns-25-heres-how-its-business-stacks-up-against-rivals-cnn-and-msnbc/?sh=65947e461b08

Mercola, Joseph. "How Linoleic Acid Wrecks Your Health," *Dr. Mercola's Censored Library* Substack, Nov. 15, 2021: https://takecontrol.substack.com/p/linoleic-acid-health-effects

Mercola, Joseph. "The Great Reset's Processed Food Agenda is Unsustainable, Unhealthy and Environmentally Destructive," *LifeSite* Sept. 15, 2022: https://www.lifesitenews.com/opinion/the-great-resets-processed-food-agenda-is-unsustainable-unhealthy-and-environmentally-destructive/

REFERENCES

Merriam-Webster. "Utility Definition & Meaning," Merriam-Webster Dictionary. Accessed Aug. 2, 2023: https://www.merriam-webster.com/dictionary/utility

Messari.io. "Bitcoin: Market Data." Accessed Jul. 24, 2023 https://messari.io/asset/bitcoin/metrics/all

Messerli, Franz H., Messerli, Adrian W., and Lüscher, Thomas F.. "Eisenhower's Billion-Dollar Heart Attack — 50 Years Later," *New England Journal of Medicine* 353 (Sept. 2005): 1205-1207.

Morgan, Gabriel. "These Energy Star Appliances We Tested Will Save You Money," *USA Today*, May 5, 2023: https://usatoday.com/story/money/reviewed/2023/05/05/these-energy-star-appliances-we-tested-will-save-you-money/70180457007/

Mulvey, Rick. "Fidelity Predicts $1 Billion Bitcoin," *Medium*, Sept. 21, 2021: https://medium.com/coinmonks/fidelity-predicts-1-billion-bitcoin-db635f226195

Myers, Jesse. "Bitcoin's Full Potential Valuation," *Once-in-a-Species*, Feb. 16, 2023: https://www.onceinaspecies.com/p/bitcoins-full-potential-valuation

NAEH. "State of Homelessness: 2023 Edition." National Alliance to End Homelessness, May 22, 2023: https://endhomelessness.org/homelessness-in-america/homelessness-statistics/state-of-homelessness/

Nakamoto, Satoshi. "Bitcoin: A Peer-to-Peer Electronic Cash System." Available via https://bitcoin.org/bitcoin.pdf

Nakamoto, Satoshi. "Re: Dying bitcoins," Jun. 21, 2010: https://satoshi.nakamotoinstitute.org/posts/bitcointalk/131/

New-York Tribune. "Ford Would Replace Gold with Energy Currency and Stop Wars," *New-York Tribune* Dec. 4, 1922. Available via Library of Congress *Chronicling America: Historic American Newspapers*: https://chroniclingamerica.loc.gov/lccn/sn83030214/1921-12-04/ed-1/seq-1/

NHS. "Chickenpox Vaccine FAQs," Jan. 23, 2019: https://www.nhs.uk/conditions/vaccinations/chickenpox-vaccine-questions-answers/

Nieuwenhuijs, Jan. "US Government Lost 7 Fort Knox Gold Audit Reports," *SeekingAlpha*, Jun. 5, 2015: https://seekingalpha.com/article/3237936-u-s-government-lost-7-fort-knox-gold-audit-reports

Novelly, Thomas. "Even More Young Americans Are Unfit to Serve, a New Study Finds. Here's Why," *Military.com*, Sept. 28, 2022: https://www.military.com/daily-news/2022/09/28/new-pentagon-study-shows-77-of-young-americans-are-ineligible-military-service.html

O'Neill, Aaron. "Global Gross Domestic Product (GDP)," *Statista*, May 10, 2023: https://www.statista.com/statistics/268750/global-gross-domestic-product-gdp/

O'Neill, Aaron. "Life Expectancy in the United States, 1860-2020," *Statista* Jun. 21, 2022: https://www.statista.com/statistics/1040079/life-expectancy-united-states-all-time/

O'Neill, Aaron. "Number of United States Military Fatalities in Major Wars 1775-2023," *Statista*, Apr. 11, 2023: https://www.statista.com/statistics/1009819/total-us-military-fatalities-in-american-wars-1775-present/

Our World In Data. "Share of United States Households Using Specific Technologies." Available via: https://ourworldindata.org/grapher/technology-adoption-by-households-in-the-united-states

Parlapiano, Alicia, Solomon, Deborah B., Ngo, Madeleine, and Cowley, Stacy. "Where $5 Trillion in Pandemic Stimulus Money Went," *New York Times*, Mar. 11, 2022: https://www.nytimes.com/interactive/2022/03/11/us/how-covid-stimulus-money-was-spent.html

Payne, Ed. "Fact Check: Children Do NOT Receive Up To 72 Doses Of Recommended Childhood Vaccines Between Birth And 18," *Lead Stories*, Jun. 24, 2022: https://leadstories.com/hoax-alert/2022/06/fact-check-children-do-not-receive-up-to-72-doses-of-recommended-childhood-vaccines-between-birth-and-18.html

Pfleger, Paige. "How the Amish Live Uninsured But Stay Healthy," *Side Effects*, Sept. 11, 2019: https://www.sideeffectspublicmedia.org/community-health/2019-09-11/how-the-amish-live-uninsured-but-stay-healthy

Pisani, Bob. "Stock Buybacks Surge to Likely Record Highs, But a Tax from Congress Poses a Threat," *CNBC*, Oct. 27, 2021: https://www.cnbc.com/2021/10/27/stock-buybacks-surge-to-likely-record-highs-but-a-tax-from-congress-poses-a-threat.html

Pittinsky, Todd L. "Inflation Disproportionately Hurts the Poor," *Wall Street Journal*, Jun. 20, 2021: https://www.wsj.com/articles/inflation-disproportionately-hurts-the-poor-11624207206

Pruitt, Sarah. "Why Did Japan Attack Pearl Harbor?" *History.com*, Apr. 10, 2018: https://www.history.com/news/why-did-japan-attack-pearl-harbor

Raico, Ralph. "Keynes and the Reds" *The Free Market* 15, 4 (Apr. 1997). Available online via: https://mises.org/library/keynes-and-reds-0

Ranzetta, Tim. "Chart of the Week: Company Lifespan on the S&P 500," Next Gen Personal Finance, May 7, 2019: https://www.ngpf.org/blog/index-funds/chart-of-the-week-company-lifespan-on-the-sp-500/

Rettig, Charles P. and Johnson, Barry W. "Individual Income Tax Returns Complete Report 2020," Internal Revenue Service Publication 1304 (Rev. 11-2022). Available online via: https://www.irs.gov/pub/irs-pdf/p1304.pdf?inf_contact_key=c57fd4e33cd49022d814dc7b16ac1f7a16358d5485884e2f31e6019a0d26c8b0

REFERENCES

Ritchie, Hannah and Roser, Max. "Land Use," *OurWorldInData*. Sept., 2019: https://ourworldindata.org/land-use

Robinson, Jerry. "Preparing for the Collapse of the Petrodollar System, Part 1." Follow the Money: https://followthemoney.com/preparing-for-the-collapse-of-the-petrodollar-system-part-1/

Roser, Max. "Energy Poverty and Indoor Air Pollution: A Problem as Old as Humanity That We Can End Within Our Lifetime," *OurWorldInData*, Jul. 5, 2021: https://ourworldindata.org/energy-poverty-air-pollution

Rothbard, Murray. *America's Great Depression*. Auburn, Alabama: The Ludwig von Mises Institute (2000).

Royde-Smith, John G. "Killed, Wounded, and Missing," *Encyclopedia Britannica*. Available online via: https://www.britannica.com/biography/Peyton-Conway-March

Scarborough, Rowan. "Biden's Open Border: One of the Most Successful Voter Drives in Democrats' History," *Washington Times*, Apr. 26, 2022: https://www.washingtontimes.com/news/2022/apr/26/bidens-open-border-one-of-the-most-successful-vote/

Schroeder, Alice. *The Snowball: Warren Buffett and the Business of Life*. New York: Bantham Books (2008).

Schweikart, Larry. "Did Eisenhower Cause the Obesity Epidemic?" Wild World of History. Available online via: https://www.wildworldofhistory.com/blog/did-eisenhower-cause-the-obesity-epidemic

Selderhuis, Herman. "The Day Martin Luther Was Excommunicated," *Crossway*, Jan. 3, 2018: https://www.crossway.org/books/martin-luther-hcj/

Senate Leadership Fund. "Elizabeth Warren's $40k in Speaking Fees." News, Apr. 28, 2017: https://www.senateleadershipfund.org/elizabeth-warrens-40k-speaking-fees/

Somers, Jeff. "Comanche: The Most Powerful Native American Tribe in History," *Grunge*, Feb. 21, 2021: https://www.grunge.com/265660/comanche-the-most-powerful-native-american-tribe-in-history/

Sorene, Paul. "Waiting in Line to See Star Wars: 1977-2000," FlashBak, Nov. 28, 2004: https://flashbak.com/waiting-in-line-to-see-star-wars-1977-2000-26505/

Statista Research Department. "Median Size of a Single Family House in the US 2000-2021," *Statista*, Nov. 23, 2022: https://www.statista.com/statistics/456925/median-size-of-single-family-home-usa/

Steil, Benn. *The Battle of Bretton Woods: John Maynard Keynes, Harry Dexter White, and the Making of a New World Order*. Princeton, NJ: Princeton University Press (2013).

REFERENCES

Subramanian, S.V. and Kumar, Akhil. "Increases in COVID-19 are Unrelated to Levels of Vaccination Across 68 Countries and 2947 Counties in the United States," *European Journal of Epidemiology* 36, 12 (Dec. 2021): 1237-1240.

Sullivan, Andrew. "Keynes's 'Jew Boy' Quickie," The Daily Dish, *The Atlantic*, Jan. 28, 2008: https://www.theatlantic.com/daily-dish/archive/2008/01/keyness-jew-boy-quickie/220620/

Supreme Court of the United States. "562 U. S. ____ (2011) (No. 09-152)," Legal Information Institute at Cornell Law School, Feb. 22, 2011: https://www.law.cornell.edu/supct/html/09-152.ZD.html

Svanholm, Knut. *Bitcoin: Everything Divided by 21 Million*. Konsensus Network (2022).

Taha, Ameer Y. "Linoleic Acid — Good or Bad for the Brain?" *NPJ Science of Food* 4, 1 (Jan. 2020): https://www.ncbi.nlm.nih.gov/pmc/articles/PMC6940357/#CR4

Teicholz, Nina. *The Big Fat Surprise: Why Butter, Meat, and Cheese Belong in a Healthy Diet*. New York: Simon & Schuster (2014).

Teicholz, Nina. "The Last Anti-Fat Crusaders," *Wall Street Journal*, Oct. 28, 2014: https://www.wsj.com/articles/nina-teicholz-the-last-anti-fat-crusaders-1414536989

Thoreau, Henry David. *The Writings of Henry D. Thoreau*, Journal 01, Vol VII 1837-1846, edited by Bradford Torrey. Boston and New York: Houghton Mifflin and Company (1906[2018]).

Timberlake, Richard H. "Money in the 1920s and 1930s" *The Freeman* 49, New York Foundation for Economic Education: 37-42. Available online via: https://fee.org/articles/money-in-the-1920s-and-1930s/

Tindera, Michela. "How Elizabeth Warren Built a $12 Million Fortune," *Forbes*, Aug. 20, 2019: https://www.forbes.com/sites/michelatindera/2019/08/20/how-elizabeth-warren-built-a-12-million-fortune/

US Census Bureau. "Historical Income Tables: Income Inequality." Available via: https://www.census.gov/data/tables/time-series/demo/income-poverty/historical-income-inequality.html

US CFTC, "Bitcoin Basics," Feb. 2018. Available online via: https://www.cftc.gov/sites/default/files/idc/groups/public/@customerprotection/documents/file/oceo_bitcoinbasics0218.pdf

US Congress. "Congress's Coinage Power." Constitution Annotated. Available via: https://constitution.congress.gov/browse/essay/artI-S8-C5-1/ALDE_00001066/

US Congress. "Congress's Power to Punish Counterfeiting." Available via: https://constitution.congress.gov/browse/essay/artI-S8-C6-1/ALDE_00001067/

REFERENCES

US Congress. "Powers Denied States: Clause 1 Proscribed Powers." Available via: https://constitution.congress.gov/browse/article-1/#I_S10_C1

US Customs and Border Protection. "CBP Enforcement Statistics Fiscal Year 2023." Newsroom, Stats and Summeries. Last updated Jul. 18, 2023: https://www.cbp.gov/newsroom/stats/cbp-enforcement-statistics

US Debt Clock. "US Debt Clock." Accessed online Jul. 23, 2023: https://www.usdebtclock.org/

US Senate. "Saudi Arabia: Friend or Foe in the War on Terror?" Hearing before the Judiciary, Nov. 8 2005. Available via: https://www.govinfo.gov/content/pkg/CHRG-109shrg34114/html/CHRG-109shrg34114.htm

US Treasury. *Annual Report of the Secretary of the Treasury on the State of the Finances For the Fiscal Year Ended June 30*. Washington D.C.: Government Printing Office (1933).

US Treasury. "Fiscal Year 2022 Financial Report of U.S. Government: An Unsustainable Fiscal Path," Executive Summary, Apr. 6, 2023: https://www.fiscal.treasury.gov/reports-statements/financial-report/unsustainable-fiscal-path.html

US Treasury. "How Much Money has the Federal Government Collected and Spent in Fiscal Year 2023," FiscalData at Treasury. Available via: https://fiscaldata.treasury.gov/americas-finance-guide/

US Treasury. "What is the National Deficit?" FiscalData at Treasury. Available via: https://fiscaldata.treasury.gov/americas-finance-guide/national-deficit/

USAID. "Power Africa." Available online via: https://www.usaid.gov/powerafrica

van Wirdum, Aaron. *The Genesis Book*. Unpublished manuscript, chapters available via TheGenesisBook.com https://t.co/PLv3WS6vdD.

Ventola, C. Lee. "Direct-to-Consumer Pharmaceutical Advertising: Therapeutic or Toxic?" *Pharmacy & Therapeutics* 36, 10 (Oct. 2011): 669-674, 681-684. Available online via: https://www.ncbi.nlm.nih.gov/pmc/articles/PMC3278148/

Walker, Christopher. "The Hidden History of Why Vegetable Oil is in Your Kitchen Will Shock You," Umzu, Mar. 31, 2020: https://umzu.com/blogs/health/the-hidden-history-of-why-vegetable-oil-is-in-your-kitchen-will-shock-you

Washington, George. *The Writings of George Washington from the Original Manuscript Sources 1745-1799*, volume 29. Edited by John C. Fitzpatrick. Washington, D.C.: United States Government Printing Office (1939).

Washington, George. "To Edmund Randolph," Mount Vernon, Jul. 31, 1795. Available via National Archives, Founders Online: https://founders.archives.gov/documents/Washington/05-18-02-0324

REFERENCES

Webb, Patrick. "New Study Finds Zero Amish Children Diagnosed with Cancer, Diabetes or Autism," The Burning Platform, Jul. 10, 2023: https://www.theburningplatform.com/2023/07/10/new-study-finds-zero-amish-children-diagnosed-with-cancer-diabetes-or-autism/

Weintraub, Karen and Weise, Elizabeth. "Federal Spending on COVID-19 Vaccine Candidates Tops $9 billion, Spread Among 7 Companies," USA Today, Aug. 8, 2020: https://usatoday.com/story/news/health/2020/08/08/feds-spending-more-than-9-billion-covid-19-vaccine-candidates/5575206002/

What I've Learned. "The $100 Billion Dollar Ingredient Making Your Food Toxic," *YouTube*, Sept. 19, 2021: https://www.youtube.com/watch?v=rQmqVVmMB3k

Whelan, Nathaniel. "Countries By Percentage Of World Population," *World Atlas*, Sept. 26, 2022:

Wicker, Elmus. *Banking Panics of the Gilded Age*. Cambridge: Cambridge University Press (2000).

WikiMedia Commons. "Median Personal Income After Taxes," Nov. 5, 2022: https://commons.wikimedia.org/wiki/File:Median_personal_income_after_taxes.webp

Wong, Andrea. "The Untold Story Behind Saudi Arabia's 41-Year US Debt Secret," *Bloomberg*, May 31, 2016: https://www.bloomberg.com/news/features/2016-05-30/the-untold-story-behind-saudi-arabia-s-41-year-u-s-debt-secret

World Bank. "Adjusted Net National Income per Capita (Current US$) — Nepal." Available online via: https://data.worldbank.org/indicator/NY.ADJ.NNTY.PC.CD?locations=NP

World Bank. "Life Expectancy at Birth, Total (Years) — Sub-Saharan Africa." Available online via: https://data.worldbank.org/indicator/SP.DYN.LE00.IN?locations=ZG

World Economic Forum. "8 Predictions For the World in 2030," *Twitter*, Apr. 9, 2018: https://twitter.com/wef/status/983378870819794945

World Gold Council. "Gold Spot Prices," Jul. 24, 2023: https://www.gold.org/goldhub/data/gold-prices

World Health Organization (WHO). "Child Mortality (Under 5 Years)," Jan. 28, 2022: https://www.who.int/news-room/fact-sheets/detail/levels-and-trends-in-child-under-5-mortality-in-2020

World Inequality Database. "Top 1% National Income Share." Available via: https://wid.world/world/#sptinc_p99p100_z/US/last/eu/k/p/yearly/s/false/9.7425/25/curve/false/country

World Population Review. "GDP Ranked by Country 2023." Available via: https://worldpopulationreview.com/countries/by-gdp

Yahoo! Finance. "Amazon.com, Inc. (AMZN)." Available via: https://finance.yahoo.com/quote/AMZN/

Yahoo! Finance. "S&P 500 (^GSPC)." Available via: https://finance.yahoo.com/chart/%5EGSPC

YCharts. "Apple Market Cap Per Employee (Annual)." Oct. 1, 2022: https://ycharts.com/companies/AAPL/market_cap_per_employee_annual

Zorthian, Julia. "Here's What the New, Tightened SWIFT Sanctions on Russian Banks Actually Do," *Time*, Mar. 2, 2022: https://time.com/6153951/swift-sanctions-russia/

Endnotes

1   Henry Ford, *My Life and Work*, p. 179.
2   Nathaniel Whelan, "Countries By Percentage Of World Population"; Congressional Research Service, "The U.S. Dollar."
3   Robert Lund, "Horse-Drawn Carriage Industry"; James Flink, "The Automobile."
4   New-York Tribune, "Ford Would Replace Gold with Energy Currency and Stop Wars."
5   Daniel Dematos, "The Decline and Fall of Roman Coinage."
6   Mary Boatwright, Daniel Gargola, and Richard Talbert, *A Brief History of the Romans*, p. 277.
7   Jared Krebsbach and Eric Lambrecht, "What Role Did Inflation Play in the Collapse of the Roman Empire?"
8   Andrew Sullivan, "Keynes' 'Jew Boy' Quickie."
9   Keith Huxen, "The 1944 Bretton Woods Conference."
10 Gita Bhatt, "Keynes, the IMF, and the Future."
11 Sue Donnelly, "Hammering Out a New World — the Fabian Window at LSE."
12 The Bible, Matthew 7:15.
13 Edison, Thomas, "In an Unusual Talk with Allan L. Benson," March 1929.
14 Stephen Clayton, "Money."
15 Joshua Mark, "Ancient Egyptian Taxes & the Cattle Count."
16 History.com, "Mesopotamia: The World's Earliest Civilization."
17 Milton Friedman, *Monetary Mischief*, pp. 3-7.
18 Elizabeth Brown, "Feudalism."
19 BBC, "Slave Beads, West Coast of Africa, 1780s."
20 Saifedean Ammous, *The Bitcoin Standard*, pp. 56-57.

21 Alan Greenspan, "The US Can Pay Any Debt It Has Because It Can print Money To Pay It!"

22 Board of Governors, "Reserve Requirements."

23 Federal Reserve Economic Data, "M2."

24 Terry Chan and Alexandra Dimitrijevic, "Global Debt Leverage."

25 William Black, *The Best Way to Rob a Bank*.

26 Michael Bordo, "Gold Standard."

27 Our World In Data, "Share of United States Households Using Specific Technologies"; Erik Gregersen, "History of Technology Timeline."

28 World Inequality Database, "Top 1% National Income Share"; US Census Bureau, "Historical Income Tables: Income Inequality."

29 Elmus Wicker, *Banking Panics of the Gilded Age*.

30 Murray Rothbard, *America's Great Depression*, pp. 94-95.

31 Richard Timberlake, "Money in the 1920s and 1930s"; Drew Desilver, "Most U.S. Bank Failures Have Come in a Few Big Waves."

32 Nathan Lewis, "The Federal Reserve in the 1920s."

33 US Treasury, *Annual Report of the Secretary of the Treasury*, p. 195.

34 Federal Reserve History, "Emergency Banking Act of 1933."

35 Federal Reserve History, "Emergency Banking Act of 1933."

36 Henry Mark Holzer, "How Americans Lost Their Right To Own Gold."

37 FDIC, "Statistics At A Glance."

38 FRED, "Federal Funds Effective Rate."

39 Huxen, "1944 Bretton Woods."

40 Quoted in Benn Steil, *The Battle of Bretton Woods*, p. 42.

41 Quoted in Steil, *Bretton Woods*, p. 199.

42 John Maynard Keynes, *The Economic Consequences of the Peace*, p. 180.

43 Ralph Raico, "Keynes and the Reds."

44 Oliver Giesecke, "Changes in the Intended Federal Funds Rate," p. 8.

45 FRED, "30-Year Fixed Rate Mortgage."

46 US Treasury, "How Much Money has the Federal Government Collected and Spent in Fiscal Year 2023."

47 George Bush, "State of the Union with Candy Crowley."

48 FRED, "Assets: Total Assets."

49 Board of Governors, "Credit and Liquidity Programs."

50 FRED, "M2."

51 Congressional Research Service, "The International Monetary Fund."

52 Alex Gladstein, *Hidden Oppression*.

53 US Treasury, "Fiscal Year 2022 Financial Report of U.S. Government: An Unsustainable Fiscal Path."

54 US Debt Clock, "US Debt Clock.org."

55 Victoria Masterson, "What Does 'Global Debt' Mean and How High is it Now?"

56 Aaron O'Neill, "Global Gross Domestic Product (GDP)."

57 Aaron van Wirdum, *The Genesis Book*, ch. 6.

58 TimechainStats, "Mining: Hashrate, July 31, 2023."

59 Bitcoin Mining Council, "Global Bitcoin Mining Data Review Q4 2022."

60 US CFTC, "Bitcoin Basics."

61 Herman Selderhuis, "The Day Martin Luther Was Excommunicated."

62 Satoshi Nakamoto, "Bitcoin: A Peer-to-Peer Electronic Cash System."

63 Henry Thoreau, *The Journal of Henry D. Thoreau*, p. 389.

64 Ironman, "The Price History of Campbell's Tomato Soup."

65 WikiMedia, "Median Personal Income After Taxes."

66 FRED, "M2."

67 Little House, "How's That For Inflation?"

68 FRED, "M2."

69 Yahoo! Finance, "S&P 500."

70 FedPrimeRate, "Dow Jones Industrial Average History."

71 Òscar Jordà et al., "The Rate of Return on Everything, 1870-2015."

72 FRED, "Median Sales Price."

73 World Gold Council, "Gold Spot Prices."

74 Robin Hartill, "What Rate of Return to Expect From Your 401(k)."

75 Bob Pisani, "Stock Buybacks Surge."

76 YCharts, "Apple Market Cap Per Employee (Annual)."

77 Carol Bertaut et al., "The International Role of the US Dollar."

78 Julia Zorthian, "Tightened SWIFT Sanctions."

79 Ford, *My Life and Work*, p. 180.

80 Yahoo! Finance, "Amazon.com Inc (AMZN)."

81 FiatMarketCap, "Top Fiat Currencies by Market Capitalization."

82 Messari.io, "Bitcoin: Market Data."

83 Ofir Beigel, "Bitcoin Historical Price & Events."

84 Yoojung Lee, "How Many Millionaires in the World?"

85 FRED, "Median Family Income"; FRED, "Median Sales Price."

86 Jeff Booth, *The Price of Tomorrow*.

87 CDC, "History of 1918 Flu Pandemic."

88 George Washington, "To Edmund Randolph."

89 G. K. Chesterton, *The Everlasting Man*, p. 296.

90 The Bible, Matthew 12:24-26.

91 Charles Rettig and Barry Johnson, "Individual Income Tax Returns Complete Report 2020."

92 Todd Pittinsky, "Inflation Disproportionately Hurts the Poor."

93 FRED, "M2."

94 John Elflein, "US COVID-19 Cases and Deaths"; Collin Blinkley, "Test Scores Show"; FRED, "Medium Sales Price."

95 JHU, "Mortality Analyses."

96 Alicia Parlapiano et al., "Where $5 Trillion in Pandemic Stimulus Money Went."

97 J.L. Bell, "No Taxation Without Representation."

98 US Senate, "Saudi Arabia: Friend or Foe in the War on Terror?"

99 John Adams, "To Jonathan Jackson."

100 Jerry Robinson, "Preparing for the Collapse of the Petrodollar System."

101 Andrea Wong, "The Untold Story Behind Saudi Arabia's 41-Year US Debt Secret."

102 Marc Chandler, "The Dollar Rules the Financial Universe."

103 Jeff Booth, "Abundance in Money = Scarcity Everywhere Else."

104 William Dowell, "Saddam Turns His Back on Greenbacks."

105 Alice Schroeder, *The Snowball: Warren Buffett and the Business of Life*, p. 643.

106 Alexander Harris, "US Self-Storage Industry Statistics."

107 Statista Research Department, "Median Size of a Single Family House."

108 NAEH, "State of Homelessness: 2023 Edition."

109 Robert F. Kennedy, Interview on The Faulkner Focus.

110 US Congress, "Congress's Coinage Power"; "Congress's Power to Punish Counterfeiting."

111 US Congress, "Proscribed Powers."

112 Burgess Everett et al., "The Weirdest Legislation."

113 FRED, "Federal Debt Held by Federal Reserve Banks."

114 American Deposit Management, "History of Quantitative Easing in the U.S."

115 David Caplan and Devin Dwyer, "Elizabeth Warren: I'm 'Troubled' by Obama's $400,000 Speaking Fee"; Senate Leadership Fund, "Elizabeth Warren's $40k in Speaking Fees."

116 Michela Tindera, "How Elizabeth Warren Built a $12 Million Fortune."

117 Karl Evers-Hillstrom, "Most Expensive Ever: 2020 Election."

118 World Population Review, "GDP Ranked by Country 2023."

119 Tom Gjelten, "Defense Officials Anticipate Drop in Military Spending."

120 Peter Bernholz, *Monetary Regimes and Inflation*, pp. 76-77.

121 Federal Reserve Bank of Atlanta, "All About Project Hamilton."

122 Quoted in Ralph Ketcham, *The Political Thought of Benjamin Franklin*, p. 186.

123 Robert Longley, "The Currency Act of 1764."

124 Aaron O'Neill, "US Military Fatalities."

125 Amir Khorram-Manesh et al., "Casualties in Modern Armed Conflicts."

126 John Royde-Smith, "Killed, Wounded, and Missing."

127 History.com, "United States Freezes Japanese Assets."

128 Sarah Pruitt, "Why Did Japan Attack Pearl Harbor?"

129 Robert Higgs, "How U.S. Economic Warfare Provoked Japan's Attack on Pearl Harbor."

130 Amanda Macias and Thomas Franck, "Biden Administration Expands Sanctions Against Russia, Cutting off U.S. Transactions with Central Bank."

131 FRED, "Federal Debt Held by Foreign and International Investors."

132 Quoted in Rowan Scarborough, "Biden's Open Border: One of the Most Successful Voter Drives in Democrats' History."

133 US Customs and Border Protection, "CBP Enforcement Statistics Fiscal Year 2023."

134 Shane Croucher, "Fact Check: Were There 600,000 Southern US Border 'Got-Aways' in 2022?"

135 George Washington, *The Writings of George Washington*, p. 139.

136 Thomas Jefferson, "To Colonel Carrington," p. 405.

137 Jan Nieuwenhuijs, "US Government Lost 7 Fort Knox Gold Audit Reports."

138 Matthew Fraser, *In Truth*, p. 261.

139 John Adams, *The Works of John Adams Volume 6*, ch. 13.

140 Abraham Lincoln, "Reply to a Committee from the Workingmen's Association of New York," pp. 53-54.

141 Jeff Somers, "Comanche: The Most Powerful Native American Tribe in History."

142 Frontier Centre, "2020 International Property Rights Index."

143 Merriam-Webster, "Utility Definition & Meaning."

144 FRED, "Median Sales Price."

145 Architecture News, "How Many Houses Are in the World?"

146 Hannah Ritchie and Max Roser, "Land Use."

147 World Economic Forum, "8 Predictions For the World in 2030"; Ida Auken, "Welcome to 2030. I Own Nothing, Have No Privacy, and Life Has Never Been Better."

148 Ariana Garcia, "NASA to Voyage to 'Golden Asteroid' Worth $10,000 Quadrillion This Fall."

149 Tim Ranzetta, "Company Lifespan on the S&P 500."

150 Andreas Antonopoulos, "Not Your Keys, Not Your Bitcoin."

151 Foundation Devices, "Make 12 Words the Standard."

152 Satoshi Nakamoto, "Re: Dying bitcoins."

153 Alyssa Exposito, "Nearly 4 Million Bitcoin Will Probably Never Be Recovered."

154 Hal Finney, "Re: [bitcoin-list] Bitcoin v0.1 released; Jesse Myers, "Bitcoin's Full Potential Valuation."

155 Knut Svanholm, *Everything Divided by 21 Million.*

156 Rick Mulvey, "Fidelity Predicts $1 Billion Bitcoin."

157 John Adams, *The Works of John Adams Volume 6*, ch. 13.

158 Quoted in Frank Manuel, *The Religion of Isaac Newton*, p. 48.

159 Emily Laurence and Rafael Acosta, "Obesity Statistics."

160 Thomas Novelly, "Even More Young Americans Are Unfit to Serve."

161 B.P., "Coney Island Beach Crowds From July 4's Of The Past."

162 Paul Sorene, "Waiting in Line to See Star Wars: 1977-2000."

163 Carole Davis and Etta Saltos, "Dietary Recommendations and How They Have Changed Over Time," p. 43.

164 Ernst Wilhelm Benz et al., "The Alliance Between Church and Empire."

165 GotQuestions, "What are the 613 commandments in the Old Testament Law?"

166 Brian Fung, "Chart: What Killed Us, Then and Now."

167 Crisco, "Our Heritage."

168 What I've Learned, "The $100 Billion Dollar Ingredient Making Your Food Toxic."

169 Nina Teicholz, "The Last Anti-Fat Crusaders"; Analyze & Optimize, "Why is Vegetable Oil in Everything?"; Dr. Cate, "Cholesterol: What the American Heart Association is Hiding from You"; Christopher Walker, "The Hidden History of Why Vegetable Oil is in Your Kitchen."

170 Franz Messerli et al., "Eisenhower's Billion-Dollar Heart Attack — 50 Years Later."

171 Larry Schweikart, "Did Eisenhower Cause the Obesity Epidemic?"

172 Henry Blackburn, "On the Trail of Heart Attacks in Seven Countries," p. 59.

173 Nina Teicholz, *The Big Fat Surprise: Why Butter, Meat, and Cheese Belong in a Healthy Diet*, pp. 36-45.

174 Davis and Saltos, "Dietary Recommendations," p. 45.

175 Kumar Ganesan et al., "Impact of Consumption of Repeatedly Heated Cooking Oils on the Incidence of Various Cancers."

176 C.J. Trent-Gurbuz, "What Are Seed Oils and Are They Bad for You?"

177 Ameer Taha, "Linoleic Acid — Good or Bad for the Brain?"

178 Joseph Mercola, "How Linoleic Acid Wrecks Your Health."

179 Joseph Mercola, "The Great Reset's Processed Food Agenda is Unsustainable, Unhealthy and Environmentally Destructive."

180 Jules Bernstein, "America's Most Widely Consumed Cooking Oil Causes Genetic Changes in the Brain."

181 Saifedean Ammous, *The Fiat Standard*, pp. 111-46.

ENDNOTES

182 Patrick Webb, "New Study Finds Zero Amish Children Diagnosed with Cancer, Diabetes or Autism."

183 Jeffrey Kluger, "Amish People Stay Healthy in Old Age. Here's Their Secret."

184 Paige Pfleger, "How the Amish Live Uninsured But Stay Healthy."

185 Chris Edwards, "The Hidden Cost of Our Huge Problem With Obesity."

186 Drew DeSilver, "What's On Your Table? How America's Diet has Changed Over the Decades."

187 Robert F. Kennedy Jr., "Obamacare Changed the Democratic Party."

188 Andy Meek, "As Fox News Turns 25, Here's How Its Business Stacks Up Against Rivals CNN And MSNBC."

189 C. Lee Ventola, "Direct-to-Consumer Pharmaceutical Advertising."

190 Yujin Kim et al., "Advertiser Spending on Primetime News Throughout the Coronavirus Pandemic."

191 Kim et al., "Advertiser Spending."

192 Karen Weintraub and Elizabeth Weise, "Federal Spending on COVID-19 Vaccine Candidates Tops $9 billion, Spread Among 7 Companies."

193 S.V. Subramanian and Akhil Kumar, "Increases in COVID-19 are Unrelated to Levels of Vaccination."

194 Florida Health, "State Surgeon General Dr. Joseph A. Ladapo Issues New mRNA COVID-19 Vaccine Guidance."

195 Supreme Court of the United States, "562 U. S. ____ (2011) (No. 09-152)."

196 Children's Health Defense, "Vaccine Makers Do Not Use Placebos to Test the Safety of Their Vaccines for Kids."

197 Ed Payne, "Fact Check: Children Do NOT Receive Up To 72 Doses Of Recommended Childhood Vaccines."

198 NHS, "Chickenpox Vaccine FAQs."

199 Kathleen Doheny and Louise Chang, "Autism Cases on the Rise; Reason for Increase a Mystery"; CDC, "Data & Statistics on Autism Spectrum Disorder."

200 Theresa Agovino, "Merck Knew Vioxx Dangers in 2000."

201 Aaron O'Neill, "Life Expectancy in the United States, 1860-2020."

202 Energy Star, "Tax Credit Legislation."

203 Gabriel Morgan, "These Energy Star Appliances We Tested Will Save You Money."

204 Vanessa Glavinskas, "The Inflation Reduction Act is a Victory for the Climate."

205 US Treasury, "What is the National Deficit?"

206 FRED, "Average Price: Electricity per Kilowatt-Hour in U.S."

207 FRED, "M2."

208 Michelle Lewis, "Two-Thirds of New Renewables Were Cheaper Than Coal in 2021."

209 Dean Freeman, "Rare Earth Mining: The Dark Underside of Sustainability."

210 World Bank, "Adjusted Net National Income per Capita (Current US$) — Nepal."

211 Max Roser, "Energy Poverty and Indoor Air Pollution."

212 O'Neill, "Life Expectancy."

213 MacroTrends, "Nepal Life Expectancy 1950-2023."

214 World Bank, "Life Expectancy at Birth."

215 USAID, "Power Africa."

216 WHO, "Child Mortality."

217 Quoted in Frank Manuel, *The Religion of Isaac Newton*, p. 48.

218 Martin Luther King Jr, "Acceptance Speech."